MORE SECONDARY STARTERS AND PLENARIES

Other titles available in the Starters and Plenaries series:

Secondary Starters and Plenaries by Kate Brown
Secondary Starters and Plenaries: English by Johnnie Young
Secondary Starters and Plenaries: History by Mike Gershon

Other titles available from Bloomsbury Education:

How To Survive Your First Year in Teaching by Sue Cowley
Pimp Your Lesson! by Isabella Wallace and Leah Kirkham
Why Are You Shouting At Us? The dos and don'ts of behaviour management by Phil Beadle and John Murphy

MORE SECONDARY STARTERS AND PLENARIES

Ready-to-use activities for teaching any subject

By Mike Gershon

BLOOMSBURY

LONDON • NEW DELHI • NEW YORK • SYDNEY

Published 2013 by Bloomsbury Education
Bloomsbury Publishing plc
50 Bedford Square, London, WC1B 3DP

www.bloomsbury.com

9781441177186

10 9 8 7 6 5 4 3 2 1

Typeset by Fakenham Prepress Solutions, Fakenham, Norfolk, NR21 8NN
Printed and bound by CPI Group (UK) Ltd, Croydon, CR0 4YY

This book is produced using paper that is made from wood grown in
managed, sustainable forests. It is natural, renewable and recyclable.
The logging and manufacturing processes conform to the environmental
regulations of the country of origin.

Online resources accompany this book, available at:
www.bloomsbury.com/more-secondary-starters-and-plenaries-9781441177186

Please type the URL into your web browser and follow the instructions to access
the resources. If you experience any problems, please contact Bloomsbury at:
companionwebsite@bloomsbury.com

Contents

Section 2: Plenaries   69

Acknowledgements

Thank you to all the students and staff I worked with at Pimlico Academy, especially tutor groups HC and HD. Thanks also to Jeremy Hayward and to my fellow Citizenship teachers at the Institute of Education, and to James Wright and Jon Mason. Finally, thanks to Mike Hendry for providing a great place to write.

Introduction

Welcome to *More Secondary Starters and Plenaries*, the follow-up to Kate Brown's *Secondary Starters and Plenaries*. In this book you will find 25 starters and 25 plenaries, all of which are ready to be dropped into your lessons, no matter what subject you teach.

For each activity there is:

- a clear explanation

- a list of required materials

- some example resources

- a collection of teacher's tips

- examples of how to extend and develop the activity

- online resources including PowerPoint slides, examples and printable worksheets (where applicable).

All the ideas presented in the book are creative, practical and predicated on excellent practice in teaching and learning.

In my time in the classroom I have come to understand the pressures and demands teachers find themselves under. Perhaps the biggest of these is lack of time so in order to help you, I have made these activities as straightforward as possible. They require very little planning and necessary materials have been kept to a minimum or where possible provided. At the same time, all of them lead to brilliant results for your students, both at the start and at the end of lessons.

How to use the book

All the starters and plenaries in this book are tried and tested and ready-to-use. Simply add in the content which is appropriate for your lesson, and away you go. If you do want to edit and alter them though, that possibility is open too. Simply start from what is provided and work out how the activity will best suit you and your students. The ideas are there

– they are creative, practical and proven to work – but they are also flexible and open to alteration. It is your professional judgement which will lead the way.

Each of the activities is a separate entity – they do not need to be linked together over a series of lessons and nor do certain starters go with certain plenaries. Anything can be used in conjunction with anything else. This will give you plenty of flexibility and make it easier for you to plan your lessons.

Below is some more detail about what appears in each activity:

- *Materials required:* A list of all the materials that are needed in order to run the activity are listed, including PowerPoint slides and worksheets.

- *Activity explanation:* Each activity starts with a detailed explanation of how to run the starter or plenary, including what to prepare and how to organize your classroom. Some explanations include a number of different options for how you could run the activity and some offer simple and complex methods depending on how much time you have available to prepare and run the activity.

- *Examples and resources:* The boxed material provides either worked examples of the activity taken from real lessons or resources that you can use to run the activity, e.g. question prompts, success criteria, key words and definitions, poetry and more.

- *Teacher's tips:* The teacher's tips boxes offer advice on how to run the activity most efficiently and highlights any parts of the activity that might be challenging, offering tips on how to avoid and overcome any problems. The boxes also include further context for when it is best to use the specific activity and the learning outcomes for students.

- *Extentions:* The extentions offer ideas for how you can extend or change the main activity described; ideas for how to make it longer, shorter, more or less complicated or challenging.

- *Developments:* The developments section offers alternative activities; they are based on the main activity described but provide different ways for running it or put a different spin on it.

  The teachers tips, extentions and developments section also offer advice on how you can differentiate your activities; how you can stretch your most able students and simplify the activities for any students who are struggling, whilst getting the whole class involved in the same activity.

- *Online resources:* There are resources available online for you to use to prepare and run the starter or plenary, including PowerPoints and extra examples and resources. To access this material go to www.bloomsbury.com/more-secondary-starters-and-plenaries-9781441177186 and follow the instructions.

All that is left to say is that I hope you and your students enjoy the activities in this book and that they help you to plan creative lessons while also saving precious time.

Mike Gershon

Section 1
Starters

Starter 1

What's the topic?

Students conduct interviews to find out what the lesson is about.

Materials required: A sheet containing information about the topic (provide enough so that every other student in the class has a copy).

Activity

Students work in pairs. One member of each pair is given the sheet containing information on the topic and the other student then has to interview their partner in order to find out what the lesson is about.

Tell the class that they will be given two minutes in which to conduct their interviews. During this time, the students who are the interviewers will need to make notes on what their partners reveal to them.

When the time is up, ask a series of students to share with the whole class what it is they found out and collate the results on the board. Next, ask the students who did not have the information sheets to suggest what they think the lesson topic is. They must give reasons and refer to evidence when answering. Finally, ask students to return to their pairs. Students with the information sheets then reveal these to their partners and a brief discussion ensues.

Teacher's tips

Some students may struggle to develop a suitable set of questions to use for interviewing. There are three ways to deal with this:

1. Put any students who you think might particularly struggle with coming up with interview questions in the role of interviewee, in charge of the information sheet.

2. Provide students with a ready-made set of questions that they can work through (see the example on the next page).

3. Before handing out the information sheets, ask pairs to work together to come up with questions that an interviewer could ask. By working together, it is likely that students will produce a greater range of questions.

Here is a set of interview questions that you can use to help students who are having trouble coming up with any on their own:

Interview questions

- Have we covered the topic before?

- What do you think is most interesting about this topic?

- Does the topic involve new key words?

- Why might this topic be relevant?

- What are the three most important things about the topic, based on the information sheet?

Extensions

- Limit the interviewers to a certain number of questions (for example, three). This will have two effects: first, students will have to think carefully about what questions they are going to ask; second, they will have to reason from a smaller base of information.

- Limit the amount that interviewees can say. For example, only allow them to answer using 'yes' or 'no'. This will make the activity akin to the classic game '20 questions'. Students who are interviewing will have to think carefully about what questions they are asking, as well as about the way in which the various answers connect together.

- Ask the interviewees to communicate through a medium other than talking. This could involve, for example, drawing, miming or gesturing. Both students will have to think carefully in this scenario. The interviewees will have to consider how to translate the information on their sheets, and the interviewer will have to think critically in order to decipher this.

Developments

- Give different pairs different information sheets. These could contain things which are relevant to different parts of the lesson. Once the first interviews have been conducted, interviewers stand up and find another partner. Further interviews take place until each student believes they have a reasonably good overview of the whole lesson.

- Invite one or two students to the front of the class and provide them with the information sheet. Next, ask the whole class to interview the student(s) in order to try and find out what the lesson is about.

Starter 2

Would I lie to you?

Students have to use their existing knowledge to work out what is true and what is false.

Materials required: A PowerPoint or interactive whiteboard (IWB) slide containing a series of statements about the present topic (some of these statements should be true, and some should be false).

Activity

Present students with a PowerPoint or IWB slide containing a series of six statements about the topic you are currently teaching. Some of these statements should be true and some of these statements should be false.

Here is an example from a history lesson on World War Two. The statements are based on work which students would have done in preceding lessons:

Statements: true or false?

1. Hitler invaded Poland before he occupied Czechoslovakia (false).

2. When Churchill became Prime Minister, not everyone in parliament was convinced it was the right choice.

3. The Soviet Union had a major influence on the course of the war.

4. The Allies were victorious in Japan before they were in Europe (false).

5. More than 100 million people served in military units during the war.

Answers 1: False, 2: True, 3: True, 4: False, 5: True

Invite students to work with the person sitting next to them. Each pair should go through the series of statements and assess whether they believe them to be true or false. In each case, students must discuss the statement and come up with an explanation as to why they believe it is true or false. These explanations should reference knowledge and understanding developed over the course of previous lessons.

After three or four minutes, call the class back together. Ask one of the pairs to explain which statements they think are lies and the reasoning behind their choices. When the answer has been given, develop a discussion in which other pairs contribute their thoughts, explaining why they agree or disagree. Finally, reveal to students which statements are true and which are false. The revelation can be supplemented by some further explanation from the teacher.

Teacher's tips

This activity is an excellent way for you to gauge how much students recall from previous lessons. At the same time, it is a good way of reminding them of what has previously been studied. In this way, the starter can help to quickly draw students back into the subject. This is particularly useful if they have arrived at your lesson from break or lunchtime.

Encourage students to discuss the reasoning behind their identifications of truthful and false statements. This will allow you to listen in to the thought processes they are using to make decisions. In turn, you can use this information to identify common misconceptions – both in terms of factual recall and in terms of reasoning.

Extensions

- Challenge students to write a paragraph in which they must justify the choices they have made. Encourage them to include reasoning, evidence and examples in their answers.

- Ask students to identify how the incorrect statements would need to be altered in order for them to be accepted as true. Push students' thinking further by challenging them to develop multiple ways in which a statement could be altered so as to be seen as true.

Developments

- Ask students to work in pairs to come up with their own series of statements (a set number of which are false). Then join the pairs into groups of four and tell each pair to test the other on their statements.

- Students work in pairs: one student in each pair receives a handout containing a series of statements, some of which are false (these are indicated on the sheet). The student then reads out the statements to their partner, who must try to work out the falsehoods.

Starter 3

List-o-mania

Students achieve success by listing everything they know about a topic.

Materials required: PowerPoint or IWB slide stating the lists students are to make.

Activity

Display a slide on the board which indicates the lesson topic. Students are asked to work individually to produce a list of everything they already know which links to the topic. This takes place in silence and should last for between one and two minutes.

When students have created their lists, you have three options of how to run the rest of the activity:

1. Choose one student to be a scribe and invite him/her to the front of the class. Give him/her a pen and ask him/her to note down on the whiteboard the answers given by students. Choose a range of students, each of whom contributes two items from their list. In this way, a whole-class list is created.

2. Ask students to team up with the person sat next to them. Pairs should share their lists and add anything which they have not already got. After a minute of sharing has passed, ask pairs to get into groups of four and to repeat the process.

3. Invite students to stand up and walk around the room with their lists. They should try to speak to as many of their peers as possible, in order to find new things which they can add to their own lists.

Below is a list that a student might make:

List-o-mania

Things I know about connected to lakes:

Water	Rivers	The Great Lakes	Watersports
Fishing	Countryside	Holidays	Loch Ness
Fish	Lake District	Boats	

Teacher's tips

This activity is great for ensuring that all students in a class experience success. Listing is a simple cognitive process which all students can access. Therefore, it is a good starter for engaging and motivating mixed-ability classes. In addition, the lists that students produce individually will give you an insight into their existing knowledge. You will be able to use this information to influence your planning and teaching.

Extending the activity from the individual student outward, through one of the three methods detailed on the previous page, means that each student has the opportunity to expand and develop their existing knowledge. An added benefit of this approach is that it helps to build a sense of collaboration in the classroom – students are constructing knowledge and learning together.

Finally, it is worth noting that the lists students produce in this starter are of great help to them through the course of the lesson. First, they bring appropriate ideas and recollections to the forefront of students' minds which makes it easier for them to access and engage with the lesson content; second, students can refer to their lists during the lesson, using them as an aid for writing, speaking and thinking.

Extensions

- Challenge students to rank the words in their list according to some sort of criteria such as: from most to least important; from most to least relevant; from most to least useful.

- Ask students to sort their list into a series of categories. You could provide these, or you could invite students to think up their own categories (further increasing the level of challenge).

Development

- Instead of asking students to create a list without any restrictions, ask them to create a list in which they have one word which connects to the topic for each letter of the alphabet. This is more difficult and so it is best to let students work in pairs or threes. The first team to get all 26 should call out; they then read their list to the class, who listen carefully and challenge any words they think have a tenuous connection.

Starter 4

Stepped questions

Students experience an increasing level of difficulty through a series of questions.

Materials required: Either a PowerPoint or IWB slide containing the questions, or a handout on which the questions are written.

Activity

Display a slide containing a series of questions which gradually increase in difficulty. Alternatively, give students a handout on which the questions are written.

The questions are like steps carved into a hillside: the first ones are near the ground and are easy to access, the later ones are higher up and rely on students having successfully negotiated the first ones. Questions should be connected to the topic and will ideally reference work done in the previous lesson.

A great tool for ordering questions is Bloom's Taxonomy of Educational Objectives. This places cognitive processes central to classroom learning in a hierarchy as exemplified below:

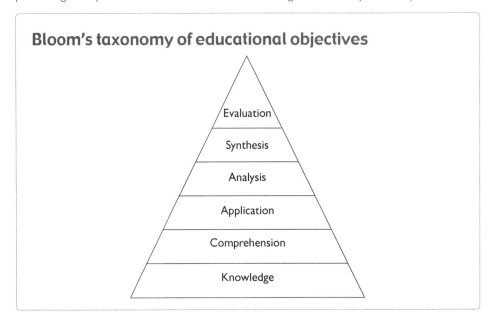

Bloom's taxonomy of educational objectives

- Evaluation
- Synthesis
- Analysis
- Application
- Comprehension
- Knowledge

So, when creating your set of questions, you can ensure they gradually increase in difficulty by having each one connect to a level of the taxonomy.

Below is an example of a set of stepped questions based on the topic 'human rights'. The first question is based on knowledge as it simply asks students to recall something. The second question is based on comprehension: students have to show their understanding. The third question asks students to apply their knowledge and understanding. The fourth seeks some analysis and the fifth asks for evaluation. As you will note, the questions get progressively more challenging.

Stepped questions: human rights

1. What human rights can you remember?

2. What is the definition of a human right?

3. How might the idea of human rights be used by a government?

4. Why might some people reject the idea of human rights?

5. Do you think human rights are a good thing? Why?

Five questions plus an extension (see the next page) is a sound number to use. This ensures that all students have plenty to go on and is a good number to ensure engagement and motivation are maintained. It is best to have students working individually at first to allow them to develop their own thinking and writing. Once students have some answers written down, then they can discuss their thoughts (and potentially amend their writing) with the person sitting next to them.

Teacher's tips

This starter activity is a great way to ensure students achieve success whilst also being challenged. Everyone in the class will be able to deal easily with the first couple of questions; the last three will prove more challenging. This means that students who are at different points with their learning will still be engaged. For example, a high-ability student may breeze through the first four questions before writing a lengthy, discursive response to question five. Similarly, a less able student might spend a long period of time thinking about question three before coming up with an answer. The beauty of the activity is that both type of students will be making progress and thinking carefully about the topic, just at a pace which suits them.

A second point to note is that, when it comes to the more difficult questions, you might want to encourage students to work in pairs if you pick up on the fact that lots of people in the class are having difficulties. This is a judgement you will need to make in context

– sometimes it will be appropriate, sometimes not. The key thing to ask yourself is: 'Are the majority of the class struggling?' If the answer is yes, step in and encourage paired discussion. This will help students to articulate their ideas, in turn making it easier for them to produce a written response.

For a list of key words connected to each level of Bloom's Taxonomy, see my free resource at www.tes.co.uk/resources and search for 'The Bloom Buster'.

Extensions

• Set an extension question in which you ask students to create something connected to the topic. This is making use of the 'synthesis' level of Bloom's Taxonomy. Here is an example, based on the questions suggested on the previous page: Create an advert selling the benefits of human rights to countries whose governments routinely ignore them.

• Ask students to come up with an alternative set of questions about the topic. Specify that these must also gradually increase in difficulty.

• When students have finished the questions, invite them to walk around the room and to find a partner with whom they then share their answers. Indicate that if, as a result of their discussion, the student's views have altered, they should return to their seat and amend what they have written.

Starter 5

What do you want to know?

A starter in which students lead the way by deciding what it is they want to find out.

Materials required: A PowerPoint or IWB slide; some multi-purpose tack; half as many slips of paper as there are students in the class.

Activity

Display the topic title on the board along with some explanatory information (this can be as little as a couple of sentences – the point is to provide some context in case students have never come across it before). Here is an example of what you might put on the opening slide:

> ### What do you want to know?
>
> **Topic:** Packaging design
>
> Explanatory information: Packaging design includes all sorts of different products, from food to electrical items, DVDs to drinks. Any product that comes in packaging must first have that packaging designed. It has a big impact on whether the product sells, whether people want to buy it and what people think about it.

Ask students to think about the topic and to make some brief notes covering what they already know. These notes could be in the form of a list, a spider diagram or a summary paragraph.

Next, explain to students that they are going to help shape the course of the lesson. Ask them to come up with three questions about the topic which they would like to have answered. Give one or two minutes for this, with students writing down their questions. Then, invite students to share their questions with the person sitting next to them.

Now ask pairs to agree on one question they would like to put forward to the class. Hand out the slips of paper – one per pair – and each pair writes their question down. They then use the tack to stick this question to the board.

Finally, group together similar questions and then read out the different options. The class vote on which questions they would like to focus on during the course of the lesson.

How many are chosen is up to you and will be dependent on the time you have available. Generally speaking, one or two questions will suffice for a lesson between 35 and 60 minutes long.

Teacher's tips

A great advantage of this starter is that it gives students a real sense of ownership over their learning. By encouraging students to construct and then choose a question for investigation, you are allowing them to dictate the direction of the lesson. Of course, the likelihood is that what they want to find out will be encompassed in your planning anyway – but they don't need to know that!

Another benefit of this activity is that students are motivated to engage with the ideas or information you plan to teach them about. Coming up with questions involves manipulating information, formulating ideas and testing out different alternatives. All these processes see students thinking actively about the topic.

If you have a large number of students in your class, I would advise setting up groups of three rather than pairs. This will result in fewer questions being proposed, meaning that the question selection part of the starter will be easier for you to manage.

Extension

- Before students get into pairs, ask them to choose what they believe is their best question. They should then write a paragraph advocating that question. This requires high-level thinking as students are compelled to consider the reasons and evidence which could be used to support their own preferences.

Developments

- Instead of asking pairs to attach their questions to the board, ask them to place them in an empty box at the front of the class. When all the questions are in, choose a student to pick one out at random. That question is then followed up during the lesson.

- Collect the questions in and ask students to get into groups of four. Hand out a selection of the questions at random – one per group. The first activity in the lesson then involves each group researching the question they have been given. The second activity entails groups sharing their findings. This is a good way of creating a coherent lesson which 'flows' directly out of the starter.

Starter 6

What if?

Students think creatively in order to imagine a 'what if' scenario.

Materials required: PowerPoint or IWB slide; an open mind.

Activity

Students are presented with a slide which asks them to imagine 'What if…?' They are given a range of options through which to respond: comic strip, image, creative writing, non-fiction writing or poem. Ask students to choose one of the methods through which to create an answer to the question. Then explain that students can be as imaginative as they like, but that there is one caveat: everybody must be able to offer a reasoned explanation of why their idea might be possible, or how it might come about.

Here is an example to demonstrate how this section of the starter works, providing text for the opening slide:

What if?

Topic: Religious ethics

What if…there were no rules about what you can and cannot do?

Develop an answer to the question using one of the following methods: comic strip, image, creative writing, two-paragraph summary or poem.

It is best to give students around five minutes to complete their responses. This length of time will allow them to flesh out what are likely to begin as nascent ideas. If any students finish their answer before the time is up, ask them to choose a second response method through which to create another answer.

When the time is up, invite students to get into groups of three. Each student should take it in turns to present and explain their idea to the rest of their group. Once this is done, a discussion should ensue around the question: 'Which of the responses are most likely and why?' You can display this question on the board so as to keep students on track.

Finally, draw the class back together and begin a whole-class discussion in which a number of groups are asked to share their ideas. You can use these as a starting point for getting students to think carefully about the topic. For example, you and other students can question the likelihood and validity of the answers which groups have produced.

Here are some examples of how you might use 'What if' as a question stem:

'What if' questions

- What if…something was not the case?

- What if…something was different from how it is?

- What if…something had happened that didn't?

- What if…something had never happened?

- What if…something changed?

Use these question formats to create topic specific 'What if' questions. For example:

- What if rules did not exist?

- What if rules were made by children instead of adults?

- What if Johnny had broken the rules?

- What if the rule about not wearing coats had never been invented?

- What if the rules changed?

Teacher's tips

This activity is an excellent way to get students thinking creatively. The question stem 'What if' opens up a wide range of possibilities, which students are free to explore in their responses. Further, by providing different options for the medium of students' answers, you are both differentiating and increasing the scope for creative thinking.

It may be the case that some of your students struggle to think beyond what they already know or assume. If this is the case, use simple questioning in order to help them develop their ideas. For example, ask them to think about separate aspects of whatever is the subject of the question – by breaking things up, you will be making the thinking processes more manageable for them.

Extensions

- Ask students to write a justification of why their answers might possibly be true, or how they might have come about, given the starting point.

- Challenge students to imagine a completely different alternative to that which they have come up with. You might give them some guidance in this by picking up on an aspect of their answer and asking them to consider how a significant change to that could affect their entire response.

Development

- When students have completed their responses, ask them to leave their work open on their desks. Invite students to walk around the room and to view each other's answers. They should take a pen with them and award ticks to the responses which they believe are most creative or most plausible. Indicate that all students have three ticks each which they are allowed to allocate.

Starter 7

Match-group-rank

In this starter students have to match, group and rank key words and ideas.

Materials required:

Simple method: PowerPoint or IWB slide containing a collection of between ten and 16 words connected to the topic.

Complex method: A class set of cards each containing between ten and 16 cards, with a different word written on each.

Activity

Simple method: Explain to students what the topic of the lesson is and then indicate that the words displayed on the slide all link to that topic. Ask students to work in pairs to make matches between the words. Explain that words can be matched more than once and that some words might have multiple possible matches.

When students have completed their matching, ask them to now look at the list of words again, and to sort them into different groups. Explain that it is up to the students which groups they develop, provided they can justify their choices. If you have a class or a selection of students who might find this lack of structure too difficult, provide them with a collection of categories into which they are to sort the words.

After students have sorted the words, request that they rank them according to a set of criteria. This could be from most to least important, for example. Explain that students must agree on their rankings in their pairs and should be ready to justify their choices if challenged.

Complex method: Give the students a set of cards with the words on them. The advantage is that students have something to handle. This makes the task less abstract and more accessible. It also invites trial and error and is potentially more flexible in terms of thinking (cards can be easily rearranged). The disadvantage is that creating a class set of cards is time-consuming.

Here is an example of the activity:

Match-group-rank

Topic: Skills of the historian

Word list:	analysis	bias	sources	evidence	reliability
	critical	justifying	challenging	interpreting	utility

Teacher's tips

This activity is a great way for getting students to interact with words. The three processes – matching, grouping and ranking – all require different types of thinking and, when combined in one activity, students end up manipulating language in a variety of ways.

The order of the processes is important. Matching is the simplest process; ranking is the most complex (not least because it involves reference to a set of criteria). Therefore, the activity guides students gradually up the difficulty scale. This helps ensure that all students achieve success, but also that they are all sufficiently challenged.

The activity works well at various times. Half-way through a unit of work, it can be used to revisit key vocabulary. At the beginning of a topic, it can be used to introduce new words (including having students look up the definitions before they start to do their matching). Also, it can be used to remind students how much they already know about a topic; this occurs when they are able to manipulate the words based on their prior knowledge.

Extensions

- Instead of asking students to rank all the words together, ask them to rank the words within the groups they have created. This is challenging as the application of the criteria in each case will be subtly different.

- Challenge students to come up with their own criteria by which to rank the words.

Developments

- At the end of the ranking section, invite members of the class to advocate on behalf of their choices. This can be developed into a debate, with students trying to persuade one another that their choices are the right ones.

- At the grouping stage, reveal three or four new words. Ask students to incorporate these and see how the words influence the formation of groups and the decisions made as part of the ranking process.

Starter 8

What's the story?

Use narrative to engage students and contextualize abstract ideas.

Materials required: A story – which could be written or visual – that is cut up into a number of pieces. There should be enough so that students can work in pairs, with one copy between them; a set of questions about the story (these can be on a PowerPoint or IWB slide).

Activity

To begin with, do not share what the topic is with students. This avoids prejudicing their thinking.

Students are asked to get into pairs and each group is handed a story that has been cut up into a number of pieces. The story could be a written narrative or it could be visual (for example, a comic strip or a series of photographs). Pairs are invited to rearrange the pieces until they have discovered what they think is the correct order of the story.

Next, students must go through the story and discuss with their partner what happens. Provide a set of questions related to the story and students continue working in their pairs and attempt to answer them. The questions may relate to specific aspects of the story, to the students' interpretation and analysis of the story, or to what students think might happen next (and why).

Finally, call the class back together and asks various pairs to share the results of their discussions. Following this, the lesson topic is revealed and connections are made between this and the story.

On the next page is an example of the activity if the main topic of the lesson was the Shakespeare play *Romeo and Juliet*.

What's the story?

REMEMBER: Don't mention that the topic of the lesson will be Romeo and Juliet!

Provide students with a short written narrative of *Romeo and Juliet* and a set of images depicting the narrative.

Questions:

1. In a sentence: what is the story?

2. What emotions might have been at work in the story?

3. How much information can you get from the images?

4. Does the story have a message? If so, what is it?

Teacher's tips

Clearly, this activity works well when you are focusing on a story. However, it can be easily altered to work with any topic. If you have a process or some sort of change over time in what you are teaching, this can be written up or visualized as a narrative. Similarly, if the topic has any kind of human connection, then you can find or create a case study which is in the form of a story. For example, if the subject is biology and the topic is genetics, you could provide a narrative based on the life history of a pair of identical twins.

Stories are a good way of contextualizing abstract ideas. In the above example, students will find it easy to talk about the various emotions at play during the course of Romeo and Juliet. They may well find it more difficult to talk about emotions in an abstract or general sense. Stories provide real-world examples of concepts and ideas and therefore give students something concrete to work with, increasing engagement and helping to develop understanding.

Extensions

- When students have rearranged their story and answered the questions, ask them to identify what they think is the most important moment in the narrative and to write an explanation of why this is so. When they have done this, invite them to explore how the story might have been different if something else had happened at the crucial point.

- Challenge students to translate the story into a different medium. Examples include: from writing to images; from images to physical drama; from writing to symbols (including labels).

Developments

- Hand out different stories to different groups. This works especially well if you can get hold of a range of case studies or personal experiences. When students have rearranged their stories and answered the questions, invite pairs to move into groups of four. Within these groups, pairs take it in turns to present their stories and findings to one another.

- This is complex but fun! Divide the story up into the same number of pieces as there are students in your class. Hand out one piece to each student. Explain to the whole class that their job is to arrange themselves into the correct order – so that the story makes sense. Stand back and see how they get on.

Starter 9

Continuum

Students have to make a judgement and then back it up.

Materials required: Some form of continuum such as a long piece of rope laid out on the floor, or it could consist of two pieces of paper stuck on opposing walls (one piece of paper stating: 'strongly agree' and the other stating: 'strongly disagree'). This could be displayed on a PowerPoint or IWB slide.

Activity

Present students with a statement which they can make a judgement about; some examples are below.

Controversial statements

Prison sentences are too lenient.

Macbeth only has himself to blame for his actions.

Wind energy is the best hope for reducing carbon dioxide emissions.

It is OK to cheat if it benefits your team and you do not get caught.

Next, present students with a continuum upon which they are to place their judgement. As noted above, this could be shown on the board or it could be represented physically in the room. Whichever method you choose, the continuum should run from 'strongly agree' to 'strongly disagree'.

Ask students to write a paragraph explaining their opinion on the statement. They should then draw a continuum in their books and indicate where they think their opinion sits. Next, students are invited to walk around the room and interview five of their peers in order to find out their views. They should mark down on their continuum where different people stand in relation to the statement.

Finally, ask students to return to their seats and lead a whole-class discussion in which various viewpoints are heard. Conclude by asking students to come to the front of the class and stand at the point on the continuum which corresponds to their viewpoint. This way, every student will be able to see the range of opinions in the whole class.

Teacher's tips

This activity is good for encouraging students to justify their opinions. By doing this, they are turning preferences into arguments. It is good to make students aware of this and to stress to them the importance of combining reasons, evidence and examples in order to create more persuasive arguments.

The activity is also good as a precursor to essay writing. If used in this way, make the statement the same as the title of the essay you want students to produce. When students come to write it, they will already have done much of the preparatory thinking and development of arguments.

Extension

- When students have written their paragraph explaining what they think and why, ask them to write a counter argument. Explain to them that this is an argument from the opposite perspective which directly attacks the points put forward in the student's first argument.

Developments

- Instead of asking students to write down their views, ask them to come straight to the front of the class and to stand at the position on the continuum which corresponds to their viewpoint. Then lead a discussion in which students advocate for their different perspectives.

- As above, except prepare three different statements, all of which are connected to the topic. Work through these, asking students to rearrange themselves on the continuum each time.

- Display a continuum on the board, along with a statement. Give each student in the class a sticky note. Ask them to write their name on it and to place it on the continuum, at the position which reflects their views. Lead a discussion in which you select sticky notes from the board and ask their authors to explain their views.

Starter 10

Connections

Encourage students to think creatively by asking them to make connections.

Materials required: PowerPoint or IWB slide.

Activity

Present students with a slide on which there are three key words linked to the topic. Ask students to connect each of these words to three things that they know about from other subjects. When they have done this, ask them to identify what they think are their most creative connections. Students should write a paragraph explaining how they came up with these links and why they believe they are so creative.

Next, invite students to share their connections with the person sitting next to them. Scaffold the discussion by displaying three questions which students can ask each other:

Connections questions

- What do you think is the best connection and why?

- How did you come up with your connections?

- How might you explain your connections to someone outside of school?

Finally, choose a selection of students to share their connections with the whole class. It may be that one of the three words you displayed leads directly into the next part of the lesson. If so, focus on the connections which students have made for this word. Doing so will create a smooth transition, making the flow of your lesson better.

An alternative way to approach this starter is to place students in nine groups. Distribute the key words so that each is taken by three groups and invite the groups to come up with as many connections for their key word as possible. When they have done this, ask for one person from each group to leave their partners and to go around the room sharing what they came up with.

Connections

In this activity, the emphasis is on students being creative. Here is an example of the kind of connections they might come up with:

Topic: Rainforests

Vegetation: Vegetables, plants, biology, growing, watching television (vegetating).

Endangered: Species, animals, nature programmes, environment, rainforests.

Habitat: Shop, where you live, the places around you, the school, natural habitat, zoo.

Students would then choose the ones they felt were most creative and explain how they made the connection and why it works. This process draws out reasoning and helps pupils to think about the topic of study using their existing knowledge.

Teacher's tips

This activity is good for helping students to realize how their existing knowledge can be applied to a new topic. Often in school, what students learn in one subject is compartmentalized in their minds. Using this starter helps students to think across subject boundaries and to make creative connections between different parts of their knowledge.

Leading on from this, the activity makes it easier for students to succeed in the rest of the lesson. This is because, through their own thinking and through sharing in the ideas of others, students bring their existing knowledge and understanding of the topic to the forefront of their minds. As such, they are in a much better position to manipulate and engage with new concepts and content than would otherwise be the case.

There is one final point to note. When first presented with this activity, some students have a tendency to throw up a brick wall and declare 'I don't know any connections'. Such a reaction is a response to the fact that they are being asked to do something which is different from much of what goes on day-to-day in school (thinking in terms of isolated subjects). You can help them overcome it by modelling a couple of examples of cross-subject connections yourself.

Extensions

- Make it competitive. Challenge students to come up with the most creative, unusual (yet justifiable) connection they possibly can. You might even award a prize for the winner.

- Ask students to make connections which go beyond the boundaries of school life. You could specify certain areas of knowledge and experience which you want students to think about (for example: sport, literature or art), or you could give them free reign.

Development

- Create a wall display containing all the key words relevant to your present topic. Use the starter activity repeatedly during the course of the unit of work, using all of the key words in turn. Each time, invite students to add their most creative connections to the wall display (hand out slips of paper on which these can be written and then attach them with multi-purpose tack).

Starter 11

Get in character

Students have to think, discuss and answer questions in character.

Materials required: PowerPoint or IWB slide displaying questions; slips of paper containing appropriate characters and background information (enough for everyone in the class – characters can be repeated).

Activity

Before the lesson, create a set of character cards using slips of paper equivalent in size to one quarter of a piece of A4 paper with the name of a character that is connected to your topic, along with some background information explaining who they are and what their views or motivations are. If possible, include an image as well. You should create enough cards so that everyone in the class can have one. To do so, you will have to repeat characters. For example, if you have 24 students, you might create four character cards and then produce six copies of each.

Display a slide on the board indicating what the topic is and containing three relevant questions. As students enter the room, hand each one a character card. Explain that students must read through their character cards and then discuss the questions with the person sitting next to them – while taking on the role of their character.

When they have discussed the questions, they should write up their answers, remembering to stay in character while they do so.

To finish, pick out one student representing each character and invite them to the front of the class. These students then debate one of the questions (or more if you have time) in role, with the rest of the class asking questions and interjecting to support whoever is playing their character.

Here is an example of the activity:

Get in character

Topic: Drugs in sport

Character cards: football manager; former drug-taker; doctor; television executive

Example character card text:

You are a football manager. You are completely against performance-enhancing drugs and you believe that any player who takes them should be banned for life. You welcome rigorous testing but you don't like it when it interrupts your training routines. You believe that the testers don't fully appreciate how big sports clubs are run.

Example questions:

How should sports people who take drugs be dealt with?

Is it ever possible to wipe out drug-taking in sport?

What do you think leads people to take performance-enhancing drugs?

Teacher's tips

This activity is really good for getting students to empathize with different groups or individuals who might be affected by a particular issue or subject. It is also an effective way of helping students to think beyond their own opinions and perspectives. As such, it is likely to lead to a more rounded, holistic view of a topic.

Another benefit of this activity is that it introduces students to viewpoints which they might not have encountered previously. By using it as a starter, you will be presenting what might be a familiar topic to students in a new light. This will cause them to think again about what they already know and to be open to new ideas and new ways of thinking.

One danger with the activity is that students may struggle to play their roles effectively. To avoid this, make sure that the information you put on the character cards is closely tied to the questions you ask students to discuss and then write about. By doing this, you will ensure that they have the best possible chance of success.

Extension

- When students have written up their answers to the questions ask them to think about the following: Why might your character have come to think the way that they do? What might have to happen in order for your character to alter their views?

Developments

- Instead of having students discuss the question with the person sitting next to them, invite the whole class to stand up and mingle. Students can then talk to a series of their peers about the questions, hopefully engaging with all of the different characters in the process. While this method is more time-consuming and harder to manage, the benefit is that students can interact with more people and discover the full range of views on the subject.

- Instead of handing the character cards out when students come into the room, put students into groups first. Each group should have the same number of students as there are characters. Next, hand out a set of cards to each group. Invite students to take one card each and then to have a group discussion about the questions, with each student taking on the role of their character.

Starter 12

Defend your statement

Students have to develop arguments which justify a given statement.

Materials required: Slips of paper which have statements written on them (enough for each student in the class), four different but connected statements should be used (see example below).

Activity

As students enter the room, hand them one of the slips of paper. Explain that their task is to write an argument defending their statement. Below is an example of the statements you could used based on the topic the Industrial Revolution. As you will see, the statements are different but connected. They cover different interpretations of and perspectives on the same event. The starter can therefore be used with any topic which contains the possibility for interpretation or different views.

Defend your statement

Topic: The Industrial Revolution

Four statements to defend:

- The Industrial Revolution had a positive effect on the people of Britain.

- The Industrial Revolution destroyed a way of life.

- The Industrial Revolution is the most important event in British history.

- The Industrial Revolution did more harm than good.

Students sit down and construct a defence of around two to three paragraphs. In order to help them, display some key questions on the board. There are some examples on the next page.

Key questions

- What reasons are there for thinking your statement is true?

- What might someone who believed in your statement say?

- How might an example support your statement?

- What evidence do you know of that supports your statement?

- What might cause someone to agree with your statement?

Five minutes should be sufficient time for students to write their arguments. When they have done so, invite one representative of each statement to come to the front of the class.

Taking it in turns, these four students read out their defences. After each one, the rest of the class gets the opportunity to ask questions and make challenges. The student who is standing up has to try to answer and rebut these – they can call on their peers who have the same statement if they need to.

When the four students have all had their turn, round the activity off by asking the class to vote on which of the four statements they find the most compelling (you might want to display them on the board in case students cannot recall them all).

Teacher's tips

If you feel that your students will struggle to write high-quality defences straight away, invite them to begin by discussing their ideas with a student who has the same statement as them. By talking about their statement, students will be rehearsing their arguments, making it easier for them to then produce a written version.

This activity is particularly good mid-way through a unit, or at the end. It is a way to re-cap ideas and perspectives that have been covered in previous lessons. In addition, because the statements are handed out at random, students do not have the option of settling on a part of the learning with which they feel comfortable. This helps ensure all students are encouraged to think about ideas and arguments which run across the topic area.

Extensions

- When students have finished their written arguments, invite them to imagine how someone might try to undermine what they have proposed. When they have done this, ask them to develop rebuttals and counter arguments that will shore up their position.

- If students finish their defence before their peers, present them with the other statements and ask them to develop some questions and criticisms ready for the second part of the activity, as outlined above.

Development

- Instead of inviting four students up to the front, ask the class to get into groups of four, with each containing a student representing each statement. When the groups are assembled indicate in what order the defences will be heard. Give one minute for each and invite students to begin advocating for their positions. When the four defences have been heard, give groups two minutes in which to have a free-for-all discussion.

Starter 13

Diamond nine

Students work together to rank nine items in order of importance.

Materials required:

Simple method: PowerPoint or IWB slide indicating what the topic is and containing nine items related to the topic, which students are to rank in a diamond nine.

Complex method: A class set of cards, enough so that students can work in pairs, with one set each. Sets should contain nine cards, each of which has one item related to the topic written on it.

Activity

Introduce the topic and the nine related items. Here is an example:

Nine items

Topic: The placement of a nuclear power station

Nine items:	access to water	proximity to a town or city	road links
	wildlife	weather conditions	likelihood of flooding
	nearby facilities	opinions of local people	cost

Then explain that students will be working in pairs and that their job is to rank the items from most to least important, in the shape of a diamond nine. A diamond nine has one item at the top, two items in the second row, three items in the middle, two items in the fourth row and one item at the bottom. It is an effective way of ranking material because it presents a range of options from which to choose. There is an example of a completed diamond nine on the next page.

Diamond nine

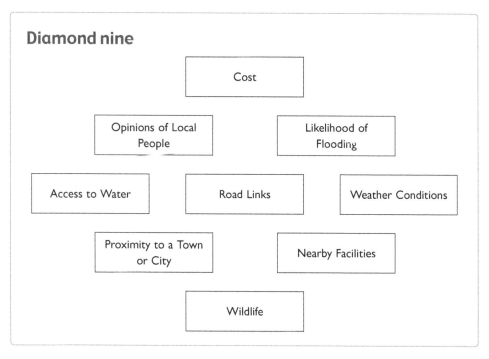

Students get into pairs. If you are following the simple method, they discuss the nine items which are displayed on the board. When they come to a conclusion, they write down the items in their book, in the shape of a diamond nine. If you are following the complex method, each pair is handed a set of cards which they then discuss and move around on the desk. When they have agreed on their ranking, they arrange the cards accordingly and copy their layout into their books.

Conclude the activity by asking pairs to join up with another group, whereupon they share and compare the rankings on which they have settled.

Teacher's tips

There are three major benefits to using a diamond nine to rank a collection of items. Firstly, it contains different levels which means that more complex and nuanced decisions have to be taken than when ranking in a list. Secondly, the middle three levels each contain more than one space. This means that students have the option to equate certain items with one another, which gives more scope for careful thinking than other methods of ranking. Thirdly, the different options and possible combinations provided by a diamond nine means that there is a lot of scope for discussion. It is likely you will witness some very engaged and enthusiastic debates between your students when you use this starter.

If you think some of your students will struggle to access the task, print off a sheet containing a blank diamond nine, with the different items written underneath. Having a sheet to fill out will act as a support for students, allowing them to give their attention over to deciding what they think should go where.

Extensions

- When students have completed their diamond nine, ask them to write two paragraphs; the first should be a defence of their top choice and the second should be a defence of their bottom choice.

- This time, when students have completed their diamond nine, provide a different set of criteria and ask them to consider how this might affect their rankings. You might extend the example above by asking students to consider how a nuclear energy company executive or a green campaigner might rank the factors.

- Ask pairs to come up with a short pitch advocating their top three choices. Provide some success criteria for this such as: persuade the audience that you are right; involve the audience in your pitch; and, give examples which back up what you are proposing.

Developments

- Print off nine sheets of paper, each with one of the different items written on it. Hand these out to nine students in the class. Invite the rest of the students to arrange these students into a physical diamond nine. While this is likely to be a little chaotic, running the activity in this way is a lot of fun and promotes in-depth and critical dialogue between many students at once

- Give students seven items related to the topic and invite them to come up with another two. This helps to create a sense of ownership and also allows for creative thinking on behalf of your students.

Starter 14

Translation

Students translate an idea or concept into a new medium.

Materials required: This depends on how you choose to do the task: you might want to use building bricks or play dough, but if neither of these options is suitable, you can ask students to use their bodies instead; dictionaries or handouts explaining the meanings of key words.

Activity

Students work in groups of three. Introduce the topic along with three key words, examples below.

> ### Three key words
>
> **Topic: Analysing texts for bias**
>
> **Key words:** bias; truth; interpretation
>
> **Topic: Grammar**
>
> **Key words:** Syntax; verb; adjective
>
> **Topic: The Romans**
>
> **Key words:** aqueduct; Caesar; centurion

Groups are asked to translate these key words into a different medium. If you have a box of building bricks or some pots of play dough, hand these out and ask groups to use them. If not, ask groups to translate the key words using their bodies. This will involve creating a mime, physical model or brief role-play which acts as a translation of the words.

Before getting started, students will need to familiarize themselves with the meanings of the words. If these are not already known, invite students to look them up in a dictionary. Alternatively, you can give each group a hand out which contains definitions of the key words along with examples of their use.

Next, students will need to decide how to translate the words. If using building bricks or play dough, this will involve constructing models. Two routes which students might go down are: to create three separate models, each representing one of the words; to create one overall model which encompasses all three of the key words.

If students are physically modelling the words, they will need to work out how they can demonstrate them using their bodies. You should indicate the options that are open to them: a physical sculpture, mime or a role-play.

To finish, ask half the class to display their translations while the other half walk around the room and look at them. Then, get students to swap over.

Teacher's tips

The act of translation involves altering something while also trying to retain its meaning. It is therefore a complex process, one which requires careful, creative thinking on the part of the translator. It is this which makes it such a good premise for a classroom starter. Students have to engage with and manipulate key words in a way which is highly analytical. By the end of the activity, they will have a much better understanding of what the words mean and how they work.

When asking students to showcase their translations in the final part of the activity, make sure you leave enough time for them to explore all the different products which are on display. This will result in two important things happening: first, students will be able to build up a bigger mental map of the key words; second, more conversation between observers and product creators will ensue. This will mean that students are spending even more time talking and thinking about the key words.

Extensions

- When students have completed their translations, using building bricks or play dough, ask them to write a summary explanation which could be placed alongside. Explain that the audience for this is any potential viewer of their work, and that it is akin to that which you find next to exhibitions in art galleries and museums.

- After all the translations have been shown and viewed, invite students to write an evaluation of their own work. Indicate that within this they should compare what they had done with what other people have done.

Development

- Use the starter at the beginning of a unit of work and at the end, being sure to include the same key words on both occasions. In doing this, you will be asking students to reflect on what they have learnt during the course of the unit. Supplement the task itself with questions, either written or verbal, such as:

    - How has your understanding of the key words developed?

    - In what ways do your translations now differ from your earlier translations?

    - How might your translations now be more accurate than your translations before?

Starter 15

Draw me the answer

Students draw their answers to a series of questions.

Materials required: PowerPoint or IWB slide containing a series of questions about the topic; mini-whiteboards if possible (though the activity can be done without them).

Activity

Once students have entered the room and taken their seats, introduce the topic and explain that they will have three questions to answer, but that they will not be allowed to write any words in their responses, they must be drawn.

Reveal the questions and ask students to respond in their books or, if they are available, to use mini-whiteboards to draw their answers. Students work individually and are given around five minutes to complete their work. It is a good idea to draw your own responses on a whiteboard at the front of the room during this time. These can then act as a model for students, helping them to think about what they themselves might draw.

When the time is up, invite students to get into groups of three to share their drawings, focussing on one question at a time. When they do this, they should explain to one another what they have drawn and why, making sure that they connect their images to the questions in the process. While this is going on, you should walk around the room and listen in to the conversations. At the same time, you should be looking for thoughtful responses which it would be good for the whole class to hear about.

Conclude the activity by asking the students whose responses you picked out, while walking round, to share their drawings and explanations with the whole class. You might want to focus on one of the three questions, or to go through each one in turn.

On the next page is an example of the types of questions that could be used for this activity.

Draw me the answer

Topic: The English legal system

Questions: What do you think is the purpose of punishment?

What factors should be taken into account when punishing someone?

How might a punishment affect a criminal?

Teacher's tips

This activity is really good for engaging all students and helping them to experience success at the start of the lesson. Many students find drawing more accessible than writing and some even prefer it as their chosen method of communicating ideas. It is good to use this activity through the course of your teaching, as it lets students know that you value different types of thinking and that you are prepared to give them the opportunity to communicate in different ways.

If some students are reticent about drawing, or proclaim, 'But I can't draw!' encourage them to start off with stick figures and simple shapes. In addition, you might invite them to use labels and notes to supplement their drawings. As a last resort, suggest what they might draw and then direct them on how to get started.

Usually in class, teachers ask students to write or speak their answers. Asking them to draw instead involves them thinking differently about the topic and the act of communication. This is good for three reasons: first, variety is the spice of life – as the saying goes; second, thinking differently opens up new possibilities and new ways of seeing; third, students have to engage with content in a way which is unfamiliar. The gentle jolt which this creates is a good way of energizing them and freshening up their perspective on your subject.

Extension

- Challenge students to include symbols in their answers. These should carry some sort of relevant meaning and should be decipherable by their peers (and therefore not too obscure). When students get onto the final part of the activity, they can attempt to unravel the meaning of each other's symbols.

Development

- Instead of asking students to draw their answers in their books or on a mini-whiteboard, hand out sheets of blank A4 paper. Ask them to draw their answers on these – but only to one of the questions. They should leave about a third of the paper blank. When students have finished, they display their work on their desks and then get up and walk around the room. Students look at the work of their peers and try to ascertain both which question it is a response to and what exactly is the answer that has been given. When students think they know, they write their thoughts in the blank space. The activity then concludes with students returning to their seats and reading through what their peers have written.

Starter 16

Find the definition

This is an active way for students to think about what different words mean.

Materials required: A handout containing a list of key words next to empty boxes (in which students will write the definitions); a series of pieces of paper, with one definition printed on each, some multi-purpose tack.

Activity

Put together some sheets containing definitions of the key words related to a new topic you are going to be teaching. Before the start of the lesson, use some multi-purpose tack to attach each of the key word definition sheets to different parts of your classroom walls. When students have entered and sat down, introduce the topic and explain that there are certain key words it is important for them to know and learn. Give each student one of the handouts containing the list of key words and ask them to get up and search for the correct definition for each word which are placed round the room and then to note each definition down as they find it. You could make it into a competition by telling them that the first person to return to their seat with all of the correct answers (you will check them) is the winner!

Here is an example of the key words you could use and their definitions:

Find the definition

Topic: Hinduism

Key words:	Vishnu	Shiva	Brahma	reincarnation
	nirvana	Krishna	Diwali	Holi

Definitions:

Vishnu – **One of the Hindu Trimurti; the protector and preserver**

Shiva – **One of the Hindu Trimurti; the destroyer**

Brahma – *One of the Hindu Trimurti; the creator*

Reincarnation – *The belief that when you die, your soul is reborn*

Nirvana – *Emancipation from the physical world*

Krishna – *One of the avatars of Vishnu, who is often shown playing a flute*

Diwali – *Festival honouring Lakshmi, the goddess of wealth*

Holi – *Spring festival when bonfires are lit and coloured powder is thrown*

Teacher's tips

This activity is a good way of getting students to think about key words and works particularly well at the start of a topic. As demonstrated in the example above, some units of work contain many important words that students may have not encountered previously. Using this starter is a great way of overcoming such an obstacle and giving students the chance to examine a host of different words in a short space of time.

The activity involves students moving round and working together. This sets it apart from the more traditional method of looking up definitions or being told them by the teacher. As such, it is engaging for students and will help to make the explanations of the words more memorable.

Creating a sheet containing a range of key words is akin to crafting a mini-glossary. Students can keep this in their books and refer to it during the course of the unit of work. This is another reason why the starter works well at the beginning of a topic.

Extensions

- When students have completed their sheets, ask them to write a sentence making use of each key word. After this, they should compare their sentences with a partner and discuss whether or not they are using the words in the same way.

- Challenge students to create an image representing each of the key words. These will act as a supplement to the written definitions and will help make the meanings of the word easier for students to remember.

Developments

- Instead of working individually, get the students working as a group. The number of groups should be the same as the number of key words. Each group is given one of the key word definition sheets and each student is given a handout to fill in. When students have completed their first definition, they send one member of their group away with the definition sheet. This student must trade the sheet with another group for a different one and bring this back to their group. The activity continues until every student has every definition.

- If you have a lot of time available, supplement each definition with a task or question connected to the key word. This will result in students completing their handouts and also doing a series of further activities which require them to analyse, use and manipulate the key words. This will lead to a more developed understanding of the various definitions.

Starter 17

Mystery object

Excite and intrigue students with a mystery object connected to the topic.

Materials required: A mystery object.

Activity

Before the lesson, select a mystery object which is connected to the topic you will be studying. When students arrive, ask them to sit down and to get their books out. Explain that you have brought in a mystery object and that the class will be allowed to ask questions in order to try and ascertain what it is and, in turn, work out what the lesson topic is.

Ask students to work in pairs and give them three minutes in which to develop some questions they would like to ask to elicit information about the object. They cannot be questions such as, 'What is the object?' You might encourage students to ask questions which can only be answered 'yes' or 'no'. For example, is the object something you can hold in your hand? Alternatively, you might provide students with some categories they can ask questions about. For example: shape; use; texture; materials; age.

You can either show the mystery object to the class at this point, or you can show them a bag containing it. If you opt for the former, you will need to make sure the object is sufficiently mysterious to sustain the tension. If you opt for the latter, try using a sparkly bag or one which is black – both give a nice touch of theatricality.

When the time is up, ask for a volunteer scribe. This student will make a note of the answers given by the teacher. Next, invite questions from the floor. Answer these as fully as possible and, after every three or four, invite the scribe to remind the class what has been discovered so far.

When you feel the time is right, ask students to guess what they think the mystery object is and what the associated lesson topic might be. Finally, reveal the mystery object and explain its relevance to the subject as well as what the lesson topic is.

Mystery object ideas

If you opt for a mystery object in a bag, you can choose nearly anything. For example, a geography lesson on pollution could have any of the following as a mystery object inside a bag: a piece of litter, some packaging, a petrol can, something which has been manufactured or a newspaper.

If you opt for a mystery object which students will be able to see, you should go for something they may not have encountered before. For example, a religious studies lesson on Sikhism might have a Kirpan as the mystery object (this is the ceremonial sword or dagger all baptized Sikhs must wear).

Teacher's tips

The great advantage of using this starter is that it creates a sense of excitement and tension at the beginning of the lesson, as students are intrigued as to what the mystery object is and they want to discover its provenance and meaning. This leads to a high level of engagement.

A second advantage of this starter is that it brings something from the outside world into the lesson. It is inevitably the case that during school life, much learning is somewhat distanced from the wider world. As a result, bringing in an object can create a novel and memorable experience – helping students to learn and remember their learning in the process.

A final benefit of the activity is that it encourages students to think carefully about questioning. They must decide what questions will best elicit the information which is needed to unravel the mystery of the object. Also, they must consider how best to construct these questions – it will soon become apparent that ineffective questioning seriously impedes exploration and analysis.

Extension

• When the mystery object has been identified and explained, and you have shared the lesson topic, invite students to come up with three alternative mystery objects that could have been used instead. Challenge students to think of objects which have unusual or unlikely connections to the topic of study.

Development

- Bring in more than one of the same mystery object. Put students into groups and give each group one of the objects and invite them to work with their peers to try and ascertain what exactly the mystery object is. They should do this through discussion, analysis and examination. After five minutes, ask each group in turn to share their ideas with the rest of the class. Finally, call a vote as to which explanation students think is most likely, before revealing the true answer.

Starter 18

Source analysis

Sources aren't just for historians – you can use them in any subject to get students thinking.

Materials required: A handout containing three different sources connected to the topic of study (enough for students to work in pairs and have one handout between them), sources can be visual or written (search online for suitable material).

Activity

Introduce the topic and ask students to get into pairs. Each group is given a handout containing three sources connected to the topic. To begin, ask students to read through or look at the sources and then to discuss them with their partner.

After a couple of minutes, display a series of three questions on the board. They indicate that pairs should discuss these questions in turn before writing down answers individually. The activity is most effective if the first question is relatively simple, the second more difficult and the third more difficult again.

Here is an example of the activity:

Source analysis

Topic: The poem 'The Tyger' by William Blake

Sources: The poem itself; a copy of the drawing Blake made to accompany the poem; a twentieth century interpretation of the poem by an academic.

Questions: How do the different sources convey ideas to the audience?

What might be lost through each source?

How might we reconcile Blake's vision – as shown through the poem and his illustration – with a literary analysis made nearly 200 years later?

When students have written down their thoughts, call the class back together and instigate a discussion around question two and then question three. The first question can be skipped as, being relatively straightforward, it will not produce a discussion with much impetus.

During the course of the discussion, you should encourage students to challenge and critique the viewpoints which are put forward. At the same time, they should encourage students to defend their views and to use evidence from the sources to support what it is that they are proposing.

Conclude the activity by connecting the three sources back to the overall lesson topic. A smooth transition can then follow, in which the you contextualize the first main activity through the sources which students have already spent time examining.

You might like to provide students with a toolkit of questions they can use when analysing any source:

Question toolkit

- Who made it?

- When was it made?

- Why was it made?

- Who was the intended audience?

- What is it about?

- How reliable is it and why?

Teacher's tips

It is best to provide students with a mixture of visual and written sources. The reasoning is twofold: first, it encourages students to think about the topic in different ways and to make use of different skills of analysis, and second, it gives students options; if they find one of the written sources off-putting or a little intimidating, they can go for a visual source first and use what they get from this to help them understand the written one.

Extensions

- When students have finished the questions, invite them to make an assessment of the relative utility of the different sources. Point out that this should be made in reference to the topic being studied: a source could be highly useful for one topic, but of limited value in the context of a different topic.

- Encourage students to interpret the sources and to make inferences about their meaning reception, purpose and construction. These should stem from the analysis which students undertake and be supported by suitable arguments.

Development

- Instead of using three sources, use eight. Pin these up around the room and invite students to work in pairs. They should go around the room, visiting as many sources as possible inside the time frame (the length of which will depend on you). Ask students to use the question toolkit outlined on the previous page to analyse each source they encounter. To conclude, invite students to make a judgement about which sources they think will be must useful and reliable given the topic of study.

Starter 19

Solutions

Students are presented with a problem they have to solve – the twist is that there are many possibilities open to them.

Materials required: A handout containing a problem related to the topic along with three empty boxes (each of which will be used for a solution). There should be enough so that students can work in pairs and have one handout between them.

Activity

Explain to students what the lesson topic is and how it connects to the previous work you have been doing. Talk briefly about how problems might arise in real life in connection to the subject. Indicate that to start the lesson students will be dealing with just such a problem, and that they will have to be creative in thinking up different possible solutions.

Here is an example problem:

> ### Solutions
>
> **Topic:** Marketing
>
> **Problem:** You are setting-up your own business and money is tight. You have allocated £1,000 for all your marketing. You need to generate a good number of sales in the first three months in order to have enough cash-flow to ensure the company survives the first year. How are you going to spend the money in order to ensure people know your company, know what it does and want to buy from you?

Next, invite students to get into pairs, give each group a handout and ask them to read through the problem together. You should then take a couple of minutes in which you ask the class if anyone has any questions regarding the problem. These could be to do with the parameters of the problem, what is and isn't possible, the precise meaning of certain words and so on. Once any queries have been cleared up, explain to students that they have five minutes to try and develop three different solutions to the problem. They should work in pairs and write down their ideas in the empty boxes on the handout.

After five minutes, invite pairs to join up with another group in order to form a four. Students then take it in turns to share their solutions with each other and discussion ensues. Conclude the activity by asking students to reflect on the problem-solving process. Ask them to think about how they tackled the issue, what difficulties they encountered and how they settled on their final solutions. If you have time, lead a whole-class discussion in which students share their thoughts with one another.

Teacher's tips

One way in which to help students think about different solutions is to give them three separate categories into which these must fall. Using the example on the previous page, we could have the following categories: a safety-first solution; a high-risk solution; a creative solution. Doing this provides students with a little bit of extra structure. In the process, it allows them to concentrate their minds on the solutions themselves, without having to first decide where exactly these are going to be situated. In essence, it is a means of scaffolding.

A benefit of this activity is that it contextualizes classroom learning through the use of real-world examples. It helps demonstrate to students both the practical application of that which they are learning about and the associated difficulties which can arise in a day-to-day setting.

The final point to note is that having a goal or a purpose is a great motivator. In this starter, students are trying to solve a problem – and it is that which is animating their thinking; that which is motivating and engaging them.

Extension

- When the student pairs have developed their three solutions, ask them to go back and assess each one. They should identify what the strengths and weaknesses of their various ideas are and then use this information to make a judgement about which solution they think is the best and why. If students struggle to do this, help them out with the following questions: Why might the solution work?, What might stop the solution working?, How might the solution be improved?

Developments

- Instead of providing the whole class with the same problem, come up with three different problems and distribute these around the class. Ask students to work in groups of four in order to come up with three solutions to their problem. When they have done this, ask them to team up with another group of four – but one which has a different problem. The groups then take it in turns to talk through their problems and the solutions they have created. During the course of this, the other team asks questions and, if appropriate, makes suggestions of their own.

- When you have used the activity a few times and students are used to how it works, throw this in as something new: specify certain criteria which need to be fulfilled by any solution which students propose. The effect of this will be to push the students' thinking as they will have to take account of the criteria when developing their solutions, making the process more challenging and more intricate.

Starter 20

Sales pitch

Students have to sell their learning from the previous lesson.

Materials required: A PowerPoint or IWB slide explaining the task.

Activity

Ask students to get into groups of four. Explain that each group will need to create a sales pitch in which they sell the learning that took place in the previous lesson. By 'sell', we mean that they will try to persuade the audience of the utility, importance and relevance of that learning. They will try to convince the audience that it is something which they need in their life, and which they should either seek to purchase or to acquire through attending school.

Give groups five minutes in which to construct their sales pitches. It is best to provide some structure in the form of a success criteria, so as to help ensure that the end products are of a high standard. See the box below for an example; these points can be displayed on the board while students create their pitches.

Once the time is up, invite each group up in turn to the front of the class (if you have a large number of students, you may want to be selective here instead of going through all of the groups). Following each performance, invite the rest of the class to give some positive feedback. Choose two or three students to explain what they liked about the sales pitch and why.

Sales pitch

Topic: Marxist explanations of crime and deviance.

Success Criteria:

- Ensure that each member of your group takes part.

- Imagine that your pitch is to be broadcast on the television this evening.

- Make it clear to the audience precisely what the learning was and why it is useful, important and relevant.

Example: Students work in groups to create a television sales pitch which tries to persuade the audience why the Marxist explanation of crime and deviance is right. In this way they are selling the perspective to the audience. For example, a group of three might create a sixty-second slot in which one member plays a television reporter while the other two play Marxist sociologists. The reporter would interview the sociologists, asking them to explain why crime and deviance happens in society. The explanations would then cover all the learning done during the lesson, with the pupils working hard to persuade the audience that this particular perspective is correct.

Teacher's tips

This activity is ideal for getting students to think at length about what they have learnt previously. It is therefore of particular use when you have a lesson which follows on directly from another and in which students will need to make use of their prior learning.

If you feel that your students might be uncertain as to what a good sales pitch ought to look like, show them an example from the internet (search on YouTube which has many such videos, a number of which are taken from television shopping channels). When you have played one of these to your students, you might like to suggest that they mimic the style of presentation and the kind of language that is used. An advantage of this approach is that it creates a great sense of fun in the class and encourages students to really immerse themselves in the task.

On occasion, you will come across a group of students who, for one reason or another, feel uncomfortable creating and performing a piece of drama. Two ways around this are as follows: first, give each member of the group a specific role and indicate what they should do, in what order and when (all that students need to do is devise the content and then run through the pitch); second, if students are really reluctant to take part, stop pushing and invite them to create a written sales pitch instead. You could then perform this on their behalf later on.

Extensions

- If a group finishes creating their sales pitch before the rest of the class has finished, challenge them to develop it in one of the following ways:
  - Include two props.
  - Include a question and answer section with a pretend customer.
  - Create a jingle or slogan for the learning that you are selling.

Challenge groups to produce a press release which could accompany their sales pitch. This should also be selling their learning from the previous lesson, but will need to be constructed in a slightly different way in order to take account of the differences between visual and written media.

Development

- Instead of asking all the groups to sell the learning from the previous lesson, give each group a specific aspect of the learning which they are to create a pitch around. Once the pieces have been finished, invite each group up to the front in turn and ask them to perform for the class. Following this, invite the rest of the students to assess to what extent the group has successfully conveyed that particular aspect of the previous lesson's learning.

Starter 21

Mystery guest

Students must try to discover who the mystery guest is, and why they are in the lesson.

Materials required: It is not essential, but if you have some appropriate clothing which you can dress up in as the mystery guest, then so much the better!

Activity

Students enter the room and take their seats. When everyone is settled, explain to the class that you are not their teacher, but are in fact a mystery guest who just happens to look very much like their teacher. Tell them that you have been invited in today because of the topic that is going to be studied. If you have some appropriate clothing (hats always work well) you should be wearing it at this point.

Explain that the class as a whole have 20 questions which they can use to try and establish your identity. Ask them to appoint a leader, who will choose the people to ask the questions, and a scribe, who will make notes of the answers which you give. It is for you to decide whether you will answer the questions in full, or whether you will only answer with the words 'yes' or 'no'. Your decision ought to be based on how much information you think it is reasonable to assume students will need to know if they are to work out who it is that you are pretending to be.

Here is an example of the activity:

Mystery guest

Topic: Monetary policy (A-Level economics)

For this topic, a good mystery guest to play would be the Governor of the Bank of England. It is reasonable to assume that students could get to this within 20 questions, just based on their existing knowledge of economics. Therefore, you could answer using only 'yes' and 'no'.

Give the class a couple of minutes to organize themselves and then ask them to begin the questioning. When they have posed all of their questions, ask them to discuss who they think you are and to put forward three guesses. Finally, reveal yourself!

In the process of revealing, it works well if you stay in character and talk about your life, experience and connection to the topic. Once students know what the lesson is about, you can stay in role and invite them to ask you more questions – this time about that which is to be studied.

Teacher's tips

This activity works best when you play up the theatrical element. Try to really get into your role and look for opportunities where you can be over-the-top, hammy or dramatic.

If students are struggling to work out who you are, give them some hints or clues. Here are three ways in which you might do this:

- Volunteer a specific piece of information about your character.

- Reveal the topic and explain that your character is connected to it.

- Prepare some images on a slide before the lesson. These should be connected to your character and can be revealed to students to help them.

If you have space in your teaching room or in an office, create a box of props which you can use when doing this starter. Over the course of a year, keep your eye open for things to put into the box: hats, bits of clothing, artefacts and so on. If you add an item here and an item there, before you know it you will have plenty of things which you can use when the situation arises.

Extension

- When students have worked out who you are (or you have revealed it to them), ask for a written reflection in which students consider the questioning process which was used by the class. They should assess this, identifying good and weak questions, things which were missed, patterns which the class used deliberately or unintentionally and ways in which the questioning could be improved in the future.

Development

- Ask a student to play the mystery guest. Recruit them in the previous lesson or at some point before the present lesson and provide them with an information sheet they can use to ensure the answers they give are appropriate.

Starter 22

Detectives

Students take on the role of detectives trying to discover the truth.

Materials required: Four different handouts, each of which contains a different source connected to the topic. There should be enough handouts so that students can work in pairs, and each pair has one handout.

Activity

Students enter the room and sit down. Introduce the topic and explain that, to begin, students will be examining sources related to the topic in order to come up with questions they would like answered.

Here is an example of the resources you could use if the topic bring studied was fashion design:

Detectives

Topic: Fashion design

Sources: A series of images of catwalk models; an explanation of the relationship between different colours; an interview with a top designer; an explanation of the advantages and limitations of various fabrics.

Ask students to get into pairs and then distribute the handouts; make sure there is an equal number of each different handout. Students work in their groups to examine their source. They have to analyse it in order to see how it connects to the topic and what information can be drawn from it. You might want to display a set of simple questions or instructions on the board which students can work through during the course of their examination.

When students have completed their investigations, invite them to come up with a series of questions they would like answered. These can be about the source directly, about specific things within the source, about things which students feel have been left out of the source, or about the wider topic.

Finally, ask pairs to move around the room and ask their questions to a range of their peers. The aim is to try and get as many questions answered as possible. Students should focus on speaking to pairs who examined a different source. These students will have information that is different and, therefore, likely to hold the key to some of the questions which are posed.

Teacher's tips

The key to this activity is providing a range of sources which each provide a snapshot of information about the topic. This way, students will be led towards questions which pairs who have been given a different handout will be able to answer. If you want to go further, and absolutely guarantee that appropriate questions are developed, indicate on the board what the various sources are. This will give students a general idea of what other members of the class can tell them about.

A good way to scaffold this activity for less-able students is by providing a pro-forma. This should be a sheet of A4 with a large box at the top and three smaller boxes underneath. Students can write what they find out about their source in the large box, and put their three questions in the smaller boxes beneath. They can then note down any answers they get as well.

In order to increase the theatricality of the activity and, in turn, to make it more fun, you might like to play suitable music to increase the tension while students are moving around and asking each other questions. An ideal piece is the music from *The Pink Panther* which can be found on YouTube or you can purchase a copy online.

Extensions

- Increase the number of sources so instead of using four different ones, use six. This will make the collection of information during the second stage of the starter more time-consuming and more difficult. Students will have to interview more of their peers in order to elicit enough information to get a rounded answer to their questions.

- Challenge students to anticipate what the answers to their questions might be. This makes the activity a little like a scientific experiment as students will be testing a hypothesis and using the methods of detection to ascertain whether what they have surmised is true or not.

Development

- When students have collected as much information as they can, ask them to write a report detailing their findings. This is akin to what a real detective does. Upon finishing their reports, students can swap these with someone else in the class and engage in some peer-assessment.

Starter 23

Dominoes

The whole class works together in a giant game of dominoes.

Materials required: A set of class dominoes: these comprise the same number of sheets of A4 paper as there are students in your class each piece with one word, phrase or name written on it, all of which connect to the topic.

Activity

As students enter your room, hand a 'domino' piece of paper to each one. When the class are seated and attentive, explain that it is their job to make one or more connecting lines of dominoes. Indicate that all students should stand up and hold their domino card in front of them so that other people can see it. Also point out that they will need to agree how they are going to arrange themselves. Finally, stand back and let the students work out the links.

Here is an example of the activity:

Dominoes

Topic: British parliamentary democracy.

Let us imagine that this is an A Level class and that we have 15 students. The following words could be printed on the domino cards:

Great Reform Act 1832; Disraeli; Gladstone; Royal Assent; Prime Minister; judiciary; secret ballot; Conservative Party; Labour Party; House of Commons; House of Lords; Reform Act of 1867; Emmeline Pankhurst; Representative Democracy.

Here is an example of how the dominoes could be ordered:

Great Reform Act 1832	Reform Act of 1867

Disraeli	Gladstone

Prime Minister	Conservative Party

Labour Party
House of Commons

Royal Assent	Emmeline Pankhurst

Representative Democracy	Secret Ballot

Judiciary	House of Lords

Students will congregate in one area of the room and start discussing who should go where and which words, names or phrases connect to which other ones. It is likely that students will first of all attempt to create one giant chain of connections. However, this might prove difficult. If it does, they will instead try the simpler option of two or three separate connection chains.

While this is going on, you should stay on the outskirts of the throng and make sure that students are interacting in a way that is positive and fair. On occasion, the excitement of the activity can get a bit too much.

When you decide the time is up (and this judgement will vary each time you do the activity), tell students to stop discussing and to hold their positions in the connection chain(s). Next, ask for a volunteer who's job will be to go through the chain and explain each connection in turn.

Teacher's tips

This activity is useful for getting students to work together and to be independent. The whole class has no choice but to discuss at length the various options for connections which are available. Also, because students are each holding one of the domino cards, they have a clear, unambiguous stake in the outcome of the activity.

In addition, the starter is an effective way of getting students to discuss words, phrases and people connected to the topic. Due to the nature of the activity – the search for links and relationships – students will analyse and assess the key terms throughout, perhaps without even realising they are doing so (if this is the case, do make them aware of this afterwards!).

A final point to note is that this activity is a great way to engage the whole class. Everybody is involved and everybody has an important role to play. As a result, students cannot help but be engaged by the task.

Extension

- When students are in their connection chain(s), invite one member of the class to step out and to identify what they think are the strongest and weakest connections. They should explain their answer, using reasons, evidence and examples in order to justify it. When they have finished speaking, invite other students to comment on what has been said. The result of this will be a high level discussion concerning the validity of the various connections which have been made.

Developments

- Divide the class in half and give each group the same set of domino cards. Invite students to create connection chains in competition against one another. The first group to connect together all their cards (and be able to justify their decisions) are the winners.

- If you have an unruly class but still want to do the activity, there are two options open to you: first, display the list of words, names and phrases on the board and invite students to create a connection chain in their books; second, provide pairs with a set of cards containing the various words, names and phrases. Ask them to use these to create connection chains on their desks.

Starter 24

Performance piece

Students work in pairs to perform an extract connected to the topic.

Materials required: An extract from a play, book, television show, newspaper or something similar which is connected to the topic, there should be enough copies for every student in the class.

Activity

Students work in pairs. Each group is given two copies of an extract that connects to the topic. Extracts will ideally contain some kind of dialogue between two people. The best place to find such examples is in plays, books and interviews. The latter can be in the form of a newspaper or internet article or a radio or television script.

Explain that students must work in their pairs to create a performance of the extract which they have been given. Students should each take on a role and then go through their performance a number of times. This run through will involve students reading from the extract and gradually becoming more confident in their performances. As they go over the piece and come to terms with it, so they can include more dramatic elements such as changing the pace, pitch and tone of the voice, using accents and gestures, and inserting dramatic pauses.

After five minutes of practice, invite three different groups to show their performances to the rest of the class. Students provide peer-assessment comments focussing on what was good about each of the performances.

The activity concludes with a teacher led discussion centred on the actual content of the text. By this point, students will be familiar with it; they will be in a position to talk about its meaning, relevance, structure and so on.

Performance piece

Here is an example of the activity:

Topic: The European Union

Extract: A discussion in a national newspaper between a Europhile and a Eurosceptic.

By performing this extract, students would be rehearsing various arguments for and against the European Union.

Teacher's tips

This activity is a really good way to get students thinking about different people's perspectives or experiences of a topic. Obviously, play scripts or dialogue extracts from books work exceptionally well as extracts, but you should not feel limited to these. Many newspapers carry interviews and discussion pieces covering many topics connected to various areas of the curriculum. Another option is to create an extract yourself. Simply write out about a page of dialogue between two imaginary characters that are linked to the topic you are studying. The extract you create can be used again and again, year after year.

Rehearsing the performance over and over leads to students internalising and memorising the text. This makes the activity an excellent method by which to introduce students to new ideas, arguments and viewpoints. In addition, it can help students to empathize with people who may think about or experience the topic differently from what they might consider the norm.

It is well worth giving your class a brief demonstration of what you expect them to do, before beginning the activity. Do this by handing a copy of the extract to confident students and then reading it through with them in front of the class. Doing this will help students to understand what is required of them.

Extensions

- Give pairs who find the performance easy different genres to work within. For example, you might ask one group to recreate the extract as if it was from a horror film or a road movie.

- Challenge students to create an extension to the extract. They should take their performance beyond the end of the text, imagining how the conversation between their characters might continue.

Developments

- Give out a range of different extracts. When rehearsal time is up, invite one performance of each of the texts. Allow time for questions between the pieces. This will mean that students can find out more about what was going on in the text and how the students choose to interpret it.

- When students have practised and showcased their performances, ask them to produce a piece of creative writing from the perspective of one of the characters in the extract. This task will see students further exploring the perspectives and ideas which run through the text.

Starter 25

Random debate

Students debate with one another but chance will decide which side they are on.

Materials required: Slips of paper so that every student in the class can have one, half containing the word 'for' and half the word 'against'; PowerPoint or IWB slide containing a proposition connected to the topic.

Activity

As students enter the room, hand out the slips of paper (folded up or face down) at random. Once the whole class is settled, explain there is a proposition on the board connected to the topic which students will either be arguing for, or against.

Here are some examples of propositions for different topics:

Random debate

Topic: Shakespeare's Hamlet

Proposition: 'Hamlet is a man who tried to do what he thought was right'

Topic: Renewable Energy

Proposition: 'The government is wasting money by investing in renewable energy'

Topic: The English Civil War

Proposition: 'The Civil War was really a revolution'

Indicate that students should turn over or unfold their pieces of paper to reveal their perspectives.

Next, give students two minutes in which to come up with as many arguments as they can to support their position. They should write these down and aim for a minimum of three. When the time is up, indicate that all those students who are 'for' the proposition are to remain seated. Students who are 'against' the statement have to stand up and then find a seated partner to debate with.

Give students two minutes in which to debate the proposition. You may want to split this so that those here are 'for' have the first minute and those who are 'against' have the second minute. Either way, once the time is up, ask the students who are 'against' to stand up and find another partner. Repeat the process for as long as you wish.

Conclude the activity by asking students to return to their original seats and then conducting a vote to ascertain how many students agree and how many disagree with the proposition. If you have time, invite some of the students to share the arguments they used with the whole class.

Teacher's tips

As you will note from the example given, this is an activity which requires students to have a good amount of prior knowledge concerning the subject. As such, it is best used during the course of a unit of work or as the starter of the final lesson.

Make sure you give students at least two opportunities to debate, though try to do three if you can. Each time students engage in a debate, they rehearse the logical structure of arguments, as well as the best means by which to communicate them. As such, repeated debating leads to higher quality discourse and more refined thinking.

To support students who you feel might find the task difficult, display one argument for and one argument against the proposition on the board. These will act as starting points for students, helping them to get into the task and giving them a model which they can follow when coming up with their own arguments.

Extensions

• Challenge students to predict what arguments the opposing side will use. When they have done this, ask them to work suitable rebuttals into their own arguments.

• Invite students to rank the arguments they come up with from most to least persuasive. When they have done this, ask them to use the results to help them create an order which they will follow in the debates.

Development

• Allow students to work in teams to come up with their arguments. This will promote an atmosphere of collaboration (within teams) and competition (between teams). It is likely to be slightly harder to manage, but the flipside is that students will be able to create knowledge together and support one another's learning.

Section 2
Plenaries

Plenary 1

Freeze frame

Students create a dramatic image demonstrating some aspect of their learning.

Materials required: A PowerPoint or IWB slide containing a list of things touched upon during the lesson or a set of success criteria (this is optional – see below).

Activity

Invite students to get into groups of three. Explain that each group will need to create a freeze frame demonstrating one or more aspects of the learning which has taken place during the lesson. A freeze frame involves the actors holding a position which has some kind of 'before' and 'after', like pressing pause on a DVD, which can be described as a tableau.

Give groups around five minutes to work on their freeze frames. You can supplement their thinking in two ways; first, you could display a list on the board of the different things which have been touched upon in the lesson; second, you could give a set of success criteria which students must try to meet through their freeze frames. This could include things such as the following: include at least two things we have learnt today; show how something we have learnt today links to the world outside of school; or, make sure everyone in the group has a clear role.

Here is an example of the activity based on the topic of Queen Victoria's reign and a criteria you could use:

Freeze frame

Topic: Perspectives on Queen Victoria's reign

Instructions: In your groups, create a freeze frame demonstrating what you have learnt during today's lesson. Here is a list of things you might want to include:

- Assessments made at the time.

- Assessments made by historians in the years which followed Victoria's death.

- Assessments made by later historians.

- The feelings of the people at the end of her reign.

When the time is up, ask half the class to get into their freeze frames. You and the rest of the class should walk around the room and examine these. Encourage students to ask questions of the performers. After two or three minutes, invite students to swap over and to repeat the process.

Teacher's tips

This activity is an excellent way of getting students to reflect on what they have learnt. Creating a physical depiction of one's learning, with the added requirement of doing so in a group and in a manner which is suggestive of a 'before' and 'after', is a complex task that requires careful thinking, negotiation, discussion and detailed reflection. As such, it will lead students to reinforce what they have learnt in their own minds.

The activity is also engaging and motivational. It gives students a chance to get out of their seats and do something physical. It is likely that this will sit as a nice counterpoint to the main body of the lesson. What is more, all students can easily take part in the activity and achieve success. This means that students will all leave the classroom feeling good about the learning – positively reinforcing both the lesson itself and the memories of the topic which have been created.

A final point to note is that the second section of the plenary, during which students view each other's work, creates a nice sense of collaboration and togetherness. Students are able to interact with all their peers and to receive feedback and questions about what they have created.

Extensions

- Challenge students to create a freeze frame which focuses on a specific aspect of the learning chosen by the teacher. This is challenging as it removes the choice from students and thrusts something upon them which they might not necessarily have chosen themselves.

- Ask groups to create three freeze frames, each of which depicts a different part of the learning from the lesson. When the time to show these arrives, ask groups to cycle through their freeze frames, one after the other.

Development

- Place students in larger groups and ask them to come up with more elaborate and complex freeze frames, perhaps encompassing all the learning which has been done during the course of the lesson.

Plenary 2

Peer assessment

Students mark the work of their peers and provide them with feedback.

Materials required: Work produced by students during the course of the lesson; success criteria or a mark scheme – these could be displayed on the board or given out on a piece of paper; peer-assessment pro-forma (optional – see below).

Activity

Peer-assessment involves students using a set of success criteria or a mark scheme to assess the work of their peers. When they have done this, they should provide the person with written or oral feedback explaining what they have done well and what they might do to improve.

Ask students to swap books with the person sat next to them. Tell each student to go through the work that their partner has done in the main part of the lesson and to assess it using the success criteria or mark-scheme you have provided. Tell them they have three minutes to complete this part of the activity. When that time is up, ask pairs to discuss their assessments with one another. Students should take it in turns and should point out different elements of their partner's work as evidence or examples of the assessments they have made.

Here is an example of a success criteria you could ask the students to use:

Peer assessment success criteria/mark scheme

- What has the student done well? Why is this a good thing?

- What parts of the success criteria/mark scheme has the student hit?

- How has the student explained/communicated their ideas?

- What do you like best about the student's work and why?

- How might they improve their work?

- What would they have to do to improve their work?

- Why would this be an improvement?

Teacher's tips

Peer-assessment is an excellent plenary as it encourages students to think about their own work in the context of what other people have produced. In addition, it gives students the chance to manipulate and apply that which they are being judged against. By giving them such an opportunity, you are helping them to develop a better understanding of what 'good' work looks like.

Some students may find it hard to apply success criteria or mark schemes. To avoid such situations, begin the activity by modelling their use. You could do this on a piece of student work, on a piece of exemplar work from a previous year, or simply through a hypothetical explanation.

Stress to students the importance of keeping their comments focussed on the learning. Sometimes, students can have a tendency to talk or write about the neatness of their peer's handwriting or the neatness of their work. This does not help the assessor or the assessed to improve or to better understand what is expected of them in the subject! Remember: always keep it about the learning.

Extensions

• When students have completed their peer assessments, ask them to go back to their own books and to write a reflection on how easy or difficult they found the process of applying the mark scheme or success criteria.

• Challenge students to analyse a certain section of the mark scheme. Ask them to break it down into smaller parts and to identify precisely what someone would need to do in order to meet all of the demands which are made.

Developments

• This is similar to the activity above, except students are given a peer-assessment pro-forma to fill in. This is half a sheet of A4 paper with space on it for three strengths and one thing which could be improved. You might want to use specific language such as three stars and a wish on the pro-forma (three stars = three things you did well; a wish = one thing that could be improved). When the sheet has been completed, students hand it back to their partner and then talk them through it.

• Provide students with a peer-assessment journal. Over the course of the year, every time students have their work peer-assessed, the assessor should write their feedback inside the journal, along with the date and the title of the work on which they were passing judgement. This is a means of keeping track of peer-assessments and allows both teacher and student to see whether or not progress is being made.

Plenary 3

Giving instructions

Students revisit their learning in order to create a set of instructions.

Materials required: PowerPoint of IWB slide containing instructions for the task.

Activity

Ask students to write detailed instructions of something that they have learnt in the lesson, or over a couple of lessons. Tell students they have five minutes in which to come up with their instructions. Explain that various options are available: step-by-step, bullet points, a flow chart, a series of diagrams, or continuous prose. Indicate that students should choose the medium they believe will be most effective for communicating the process of what has happened during the lesson. Also, you may wish to specify an audience for who your students are writing. Examples of who this might be include: students in a lower year, students studying the course next year, parents, someone who has never encountered the topic or students from another school.

Here are some examples of the instructions you could provide for three different topics:

Giving instructions

Topic: Volcanoes

Instructions: Create a set of instructions which explain in detail the life-cycle of a volcanic eruption.

Topic: Writing Haikus

Instructions: Create a set of instructions which explain how to write high-quality Haikus.

Topic: Javelin Throwing Technique

Instructions: Create a set of instructions which explain how to throw a javelin correctly, including the biomechanics.

When the five minutes are up, ask students to get into groups of three. Students should swap books and read through each other's instructions. They should then repeat the process, so that everyone in the group has read everyone else's work.

Next, provide each group with a blank sheet of A4 paper. Students must now work together to synthesize their three separate sets of instructions into one main set that is the most detailed of all. Students have five minutes in which to do this. When the time is up, each group joins up with another group. The two sets of students then take it in turns to talk each other through their instructions.

Teacher's tips

The great benefit of this activity is that it makes students think with care and attention about something they have learnt. Coming up with detailed instructions is harder than it sounds. Students will have to consider all the little elements of a process, and communicate these clearly and concisely. By the end of the activity, everybody in the class will have spent a good amount of time revisiting, analysing and reformulating what they have learnt.

One thing to watch out for is students who think they can get away with completing the activity quickly, but without much detail. During the first part of the plenary, when students are working individually, walk around the room and read through what is being written. Use questioning and prompts to ensure that all students are creating instructions which are as detailed as they possibly can be.

Extensions

- When students are working individually, ask them to highlight what they believe to be the three most important parts of their instructions. They should write a justification of their choices underneath their finished work.

- Challenge students to use two different methods of communication to create their instructions. To make this extra difficult, ask students to intertwine the two methods. For example, they could write in continuous prose but also include diagrams wherever appropriate.

Development

- Divide the class into larger groups (five or six students in each will be sufficient). Give the groups a sheet of A2 paper and a marker pen. Ask students to work in their teams to come up with a detailed set of instructions within five minutes. When the time is up, ask the groups to lay their pieces of paper next to each other on a row of tables. Students should then examine each of the instructions in turn before comparing them to their own. The activity concludes with a vote over which set of instructions students believe to be the best.

Plenary 4

Creative connections

Students make connections between their learning and random words or pictures. Creative thinking is a must!

Materials required: A PowerPoint or IWB slide containing a collection of randomly-selected words or pictures.

Activity

Explain to students that the lesson will conclude with some creative thinking. Display a slide containing either six randomly-selected words or six randomly-selected pictures. Ask students to make one or more connections between what they have learnt and what is displayed on the board. Students will have to be creative in order to generate connections; tenuous links are allowed, as long as they can be explained.

Here is an example of random words you could use if the topic was the European Union and connections that students might make:

Creative connections

Topic: The European Union

Random words: box   cat   interior   statue   lens   hook

Connections:

- The European Union is like a lens through which politicians look – and they all see something different.

- Cats being let out of the box is like a country being thrown out of the European Union – no one wants it to happen.

- The Statue of Liberty connects to the European Union because both represent freedom and liberty.

Ask students to write down connections between the topic and as many of the words or pictures as possible. Encourage them to be as creative as possible! When five minutes has passed, choose individual students to share their connections. Each time, they should explain the reasoning behind their thinking. If they fail to do this, use questioning to draw out the information. Make the exercise more difficult by challenging students to find a way to connect their learning to all six words or pictures.

Teacher's tips

This activity encourages students to analyse and examine what they have learnt during the lesson. They have to do this in order to develop suitable connections between their learning and the random words or pictures. The result is that students reinforce the knowledge and understanding they have developed. At the same time, they make new connections and observe new relationships, adding to the thinking they have already done.

When first greeted with this task, some students can appear fazed and uncertain about what is being asked of them. To overcome this, model an example: pick out one of the random words or pictures and talk through how you might go about connecting it to the content of the lesson. This will provide students with a starting point from which they can make their own connections.

When you are questioning students about the connections they have made, push them to really explain the thought processes they went through. The benefits of this are twofold: first, the student will have to reflect carefully on their own thinking and this will help them to better understand the process of learning as well as their own mind; second, students who are listening will be given an insight into someone else's thinking process – which may include ways of doing things that they themselves would not necessarily consider.

Extensions

- Challenge students to pick random words out of a dictionary, this is instead of you providing them. Students must then make connections between these words and their learning.

- Ask students to come up with the most unlikely words they can think of, and then get them to share these with the rest of the class. Select six and use these instead of any that you provide. It will be a real challenge for students to make connections between these and their learning.

Developments

- When you have revealed the six words or pictures, invite students to get into groups of three. Ask them to work with their peers to create a drama piece which demonstrates how the learning from the lesson might feasibly connect to three of the words or pictures.

- Challenge students to write a story which connects three or more of the words or pictures to their learning. If students manage to do this, ask them to attempt to include all six. Pick out three or four students to read their stories to the whole class.

Plenary 5

Story time

Students reimagine their learning, or part of the lesson, as a story.

Materials required: A sheet of A4 paper divided into six boxes, there should be one piece of paper for every student in the class.

Activity

Explain to students that they are going to turn their learning or a part of the lesson (you will need to specify which) into a story. Indicate that the story will be in the form of a comic strip and that it should have a clear beginning, middle and end.

To begin, ask students to work in pairs to identify what they think the beginning, middle and end of their stories could be. While they are doing this, move around the room and prompt students who are struggling to come up with ideas.

When students have settled on the different parts of their story, distribute the sheets of paper – one per student. Explain that everyone in the class now has to convert their story into comic strip form. Point out that the first box can be used for the beginning, the next three boxes for the middle and the fifth box for the ending. Box six should be left blank. You should also indicate that students can annotate their drawings and include explanatory text or speech bubbles if they wish.

Once the stories are complete, invite students to share their work with three other people in the class. When students have read the work of one of their peers, they should write a positive comment about it in the blank box on their colleague's sheet.

If students find it difficult to come up with a suitable story, provide them with a structure into which they can fit their learning or the lesson content. Examples include:

- How I became smarter.

- The story of what I know now and how I learnt it.

- From not knowing to knowing: the steps I took.

Story time

Below is an example of a story based on the topic arable and pastoral farming:

Once upon a time there was a farmer who owned a large set of fields on a hillside and a smaller set on some flat land. He decided to grow crops on the hillside because it was bigger, and keep animals on the flat. After a few years he was nearly broke. The crops weren't very good and he wasn't making much money. The farmer decided to swap things over to try and fix his business. The crops went on the flat land and the animals went on the hillside. After a few more years the farmer was making good profits. He had successfully worked out what land is best for arable farming and what land is best for pastoral farming. The end!

Teacher's tips

There are two major benefits of this activity. First, students have to think about what they have learnt and the lesson which has just gone in great detail. They must analyse every aspect of it in order to work out how it can be made into a story. Furthermore, by asking students to adhere to a beginning, middle and end structure, you will be making them view their learning and the lesson in the context of where they have come from and where they are now at. This process will inevitably result in them revaluating (and thus reinforcing) what they have learnt.

Second, students transform what they have learnt, or the entire lesson, into a narrative. This helps to make it more memorable and also imbues it with greater meaning. These two things are inherent in all stories. The plenary takes advantage of them for the purposes of learning.

Extensions

- Challenge students to write a piece of prose to go alongside their comic strip. This should be an extension of their drawings, going into details and ideas which they were not able to include in their first piece of work.

- Ask students to assess the comic strip they have created. Indicate that they should consider the following points: How accurately does it convey the learning/lesson content? How might someone interpret the different elements? In what ways might it be improved and why?

Development

- Instead of asking students to create a comic strip narrative, challenge them to create a dramatic role-play in which they recreate either their learning or a particular part of the lesson. Encourage students to play up the various elements of this. They should use dramatic licence to make their piece fun, engaging and memorable. After five minutes of preparation time, call on different groups to show their stories to the rest of the class.

Plenary 6

Different shoes

Students revisit and re-contextualize their learning from a different point of view.

Materials required: A PowerPoint or IWB slide containing instructions for the activity.

Activity

Ask students to think back over the lesson and to imagine how it might have been different if someone else had taught it. Provide three disparate examples of who this could have been, all of which should link to the topic. Here are some examples in order to make this point clearer:

Different shoes

Topic: Macbeth

Instructions: How might the lesson have been different if Lady Macbeth had taught it?

How might the lesson have been different if Shakespeare had taught it?

How might the lesson have been different if the three witches had taught it?

Topic: Wood carving

Questions: How might the lesson have been different if a carpenter had taught it?

How might the lesson have been different if an environmentalist had taught it?

How might the lesson have been different if a designer had taught it?

Explain that students should work in pairs and that they should note down three key bullet points for each of the examples. In addition, students should be ready to justify the ideas they have developed.

Give students around five minutes to complete this section of the plenary. When the time is up, invite different members of the class to share their ideas. Work through the examples, one at a time. If you are running close to the end of the lesson, just go with the example which you feel will elicit the best responses.

After each pair provides feedback about their thoughts, invite other members of the class to challenge them. This will involve alternative arguments being put forward, suggestions being made as to how things might be different, or critical questions being asked.

Teacher's tips

The key purpose of this activity is to get students to reflect on their learning from different points of view. As you will notice, the two examples on the previous page demonstrate how picking out characters or groups that are connected with your topic will give students the opportunity to come at the lesson from a range of angles. In so doing, they will further their own understanding and reinforce what they have learnt.

Imagining how the lesson might have been different also involves assessing and analysing what was actually the case. In fact, this must be done if one is to be successful in the task. The process sees students revisiting what they have learnt and then further manipulating the ideas and information. All of this will help to reinforce their learning and aid future recollection.

If students find it difficult to come up with ways in which the lesson might have been different, provide them with three specific areas which they can look at in turn. For example: How might the start, middle and end have been different? Or: How might the teaching, learning and information have been different? Breaking things up like this makes it easier for students. They can look at each in turn, moving on only when they feel confident to do so.

Extensions

• Challenge students to think of a different character or group that is connected with the topic. When they have done this, they should reimagine the lesson from their perspective.

• Ask students to write an account of why the different characters or groups might have done the lesson differently. They should focus on their relationships to the topic, their motivations, desires and interpretations.

Development

• Divide the class into three groups and assign each group one of the options. Invite students to work in their teams to produce a detailed analysis of how the lesson might have been different and to supplement this with a dramatic role-play showcasing some of the things which might have happened. Give the class around ten minutes preparation time and then have five minutes performance time, with each group taking it in turns to show their work.

Plenary 7

Explain it!

Students have to explain their learning to an audience chosen by the teacher.

Materials required: A PowerPoint or IWB slide containing instructions for the task.

Activity

Explain that you are setting students the challenge of explaining what they have learnt during the course of the lesson. Add the caveat that you will be specifying who the audience will be. Below are some ideas of different audiences you could present to the students:

Different audiences

- A student younger than yourself.

- A student five years younger than yourself.

- Your parents.

- Someone who has never heard of the topic before.

- An alien.

- A person from the nineteenth-century.

- Someone from another country who speaks no English.

- Someone who knows a lot about the topic.

- A student who has been studying the topic but who has missed the current lesson.

- Someone who could use the information from the lesson in their day-to-day life.

Depending on which audience you specify, students will have to take account of different demands. In turn, this will influence what they do with the knowledge and understanding they have developed during the course of the lesson. For example, if the audience is an alien, then students may have to communicate using symbols. If the audience is someone from the nineteenth-century, then students will have to provide appropriate background information before they start explaining what they learnt in the lesson.

Give students five minutes in which to explain their learning in their books. Be aware that when using some of the more difficult audiences, students may need closer to ten minutes. Indicate to students that it is their choice how they convey their explanation: words, pictures and symbols are all acceptable.

When the time is up, invite students to share their work with three other people. In each instance, students should seek to compare and contrast their own work with that of their peers. They should ask themselves the questions: How is the work similar to mine? And: What have they done differently and why?

Teacher's tips

The plenary prompts students to revisit and manipulate what they have studied during the lesson. In preparing a piece of work which communicates their knowledge and understanding, students will have to go back over their learning and assess whether (and how) they do know and understand it.

The activity is particularly good at reinforcing learning because it asks students to recreate their knowledge in a communicable form. This process sees students thinking carefully and at length about what it is they have learnt as one must be familiar and comfortable with ideas and information if one is to convey them clearly.

The final point to note is that some of the audiences listed will require students to be critical and creative in their thinking. For example, choosing an alien as the audience will limit the range of options open to students – after all, aliens are unlikely to understand English. Choosing these audiences is therefore a good way of challenging the whole class to think deeply about their learning.

Extensions

- Give students a further set of criteria to which their explanations must conform. For example: You may only use 14 words and you must include at least one symbol. This will lead students to think at length about how best to communicate their learning, given the stringency of the criteria.

- Challenge students to plan a lesson through which they could help their audience understand what they have learnt. This will encourage students to think about the processes that need to be in place for an effective learning experience.

Development

- When students have come up with their explanations, invite them to get into groups of three and to agree on a shared explanation arising out of the three separate ones they have produced. Next, ask students to get into groups of six and to repeat the process. Finally, ask these groups to share their explanations with the class. See if the entire group can negotiate an agreed explanation.

Plenary 8

In the spotlight

Students are put under the spotlight as they attempt to answer questions about the topic.

Materials required: A series of questions about the lesson displayed through PowerPoint or IWB slides; a spotlight (optional); a class set of mini-whiteboards (optional).

Activity

A volunteer or a group of students are invited to the front of the room to be in the spotlight (literally if you have one). Explain that you will ask them five questions connected to the lesson and that, for each answer given, the rest of the class should indicate whether they agree or disagree. This can be done through one of two methods: first, you can hand out a class set of mini-whiteboards, giving one to each student, which can then be used to show students' positions regarding their answers; second, you can ask students to respond using their thumbs: thumbs up = I agree; thumbs in the middle = I think it might be right, but I'm not sure; thumbs down = I disagree.

Here is an example of the types of questions you might ask:

In the spotlight

Topic: Sociology of crime and deviance

Questions: What makes an act deviant? How does social control connect to deviance?

What is the difference between historical and cultural deviance?

What might stop an act being seen as deviant? Is deviance socially constructed?

Begin by revealing the first question. You could either create five separate slides, one for each question, or you could use the animation function in Microsoft PowerPoint to make the questions appear one at a time.

The student or group who are at the front of the class must provide an answer to the question. They should explain their answer and respond to any questions you ask (these are likely to include questions of clarification and prompting). The rest of the class then indicate whether they agree or disagree with the answer which has been given. Choose a few students to explain their positions before revealing what the correct answer is. This process is repeated for each of the five questions.

If the opportunity arises to facilitate a discussion between the student or group at the front and other members of the class, take it. This will most likely revolve around a disagreement about the correct answer. By helping a discussion to develop, you will be encouraging students to think and talk at length about the learning which has taken place during the lesson.

Teacher's tips

If you have one student at the front of the class (in the spotlight) make sure they are confident with the work, otherwise, they may struggle to provide answers to the questions and this will then cause the activity to fall flat.

A way to allow less confident students to take the spotlight is to have a group come up to the front of the class. These students can then confer before giving their answers and the weight of expectation is distributed around the group, easing the burden on each individual.

As noted above, do try to facilitate discussion wherever possible. This will lead to students exploring the learning from the lesson in depth and from a committed and engaged point of view (students will be trying to defend their positions). This is helpful to those students who are part of the discussion, but it is also of benefit to those who are listening in. These students will be able to reflect on what is being said and compare it to their own ideas about the learning.

A nice way to use this activity is to repeat it over a unit of work. That way, everyone in the class can have a turn 'in the spotlight'. At the beginning of the unit, divide the class into groups and explain that each group will have one opportunity to come to the front of the class and take the lead on answering questions about the lesson. An advantage of taking this approach is that students will know everyone is to be involved. This will help to create a collaborative and supportive atmosphere each time the plenary comes around.

Extensions

- Challenge students to develop their answers in detail by giving clear justifications for why they think what they do. These should include reference to reasons, evidence and examples.

- Invite members of the class to question the student or group who are stood at the front of the class. This questioning should centre on the answers to the questions which have been given.

Development

- Make the task competitive by inviting two students or two groups of students to the front of the class. These must then compete against each other in attempting to answer the questions. Alternate who answers first and the class then votes on how many points out of five each student or group deserves for the answer which they gave.

Plenary 9

My word!

The whole class try to create a chain of connecting words related to the topic.

No materials required

Activity

Explain to the class that you are going to play a game constructed around words related to the topic. Give students three minutes to go back through their notes and remind themselves of what they have been studying over the last few lessons.

When the time is up, ask students to work with the person sitting next to them. Each student should take it in turns to come up with five different words connected to the topic and to quiz their partner on their meanings.

Next, explain that the game is going to begin. It works as follows: start by pointing at one student. This student stands up and says a word which is connected to the topic. They then point at a second student, stating their name. The first student sits down and the second stands up. They have to give a word related to the topic which connects to that which was said by the first student. They must also explain how the two words connect. Having done this the second student points to a third student and states their name. The process then repeats. The class's objective is to create a chain of students as long as possible (preferably encompassing every student).

Here is an example of the start of the activity in action:

> ## My word!
>
> **Topic:** The mass media
>
> **First Student (Billy):** Television. I pick Dennis to go next.
>
> **Dennis:** Editors. This connects because editors decide what goes into the programmes that we see on TV, like the news. I pick Rebecca.
>
> **Rebecca:** Journalists. This connects to editors because journalists on a newspaper work under editors and have to go through them to get their stories published. I pick Julia.
>
> **Julia:** Newspapers. Journalists write articles for newspapers. I pick John.

If a student makes an incorrect connection, or fails to make a connection at all, then the chain is broken and the class must start again. In subsequent iterations, the same person must start things off, but the order of students does not have to remain the same.

Teacher's tips

This activity is a really good way to get students to revisit vocabulary connected to a topic and to reinforce the pronunciation and meaning of that vocabulary in their minds. The game itself is prefaced by a period of revision and paired testing so as to give all students an opportunity to go over the vocabulary in detail. It also leads to a higher chance of students experiencing success during the game.

In order to provide students with greater support during the course of this activity, you could display a list of key words on the board. This will help direct students and ensure that they do not miss out any important vocabulary.

For students who have great difficulty with defining and memorising the words in your subject, you could create glossaries containing simple definitions allied to appropriate images. Students can then use these during the first part of the activity. If necessary, they can also keep them to hand for the purpose of consultation during the latter half of the plenary.

A major benefit of this activity is that it requires the whole class to work together. Play this up by stressing that the only way to truly complete the activity is by constructing a chain of connections which includes every student in the class.

Extensions

• Ask students to connect their word to the word which came before the previous one. To begin, you will need to ask two students to state a word. Pupil three would then have to connect their word to that spoken by student one. Student four would have to connect their word to that spoken by student two, and so on.

• Challenge students to define and exemplify the words they state. This is in addition to explaining how they connect to the previous word.

Development

• Divide the class in half and have two games running concurrently. The aim for both sets of students is to complete their chain before the other group. This is likely to get quite chaotic and potentially a little raucous. You will need to expend a fair amount of energy to stay on top of things. However, the sense of fun and competition, coupled with the concomitant focus on learning, makes it worthwhile.

Plenary 10

Bingo!

Students play bingo, but the numbers are replaced by key words.

Materials required: A half-sheet of A4 with a 3 × 3 grid on it, one per student; PowerPoint or IWB slide containing a list of 20 words connected to the topic; a piece of blank paper.

Activity

Explain to students that you will be playing a game of bingo in which numbers are replaced by key words connected to the topic. If students are not familiar with how bingo works, go over the rules of the game first.

Hand out the pieces of paper containing the 3 × 3 grids and display the slide containing the 20 words.

Invite students to select nine of the words and to write these in the empty boxes on their grids. Students usually need two to three minutes for this. Walk around the class checking that students are filling in their grids correctly and continue until you are satisfied that everyone has written down nine words.

Ask for silence and get ready to begin. Explain that you will not be reading out the words, but will instead be calling out their definitions. Students will need to listen carefully and to work out which word each definition applies to. If they have that word written down, they should cross it off. As you go through the definitions, note down each word on blank sheet of paper – this will help you to keep track.

Below is a set of words and definitions ready for you to use in an English revision session:

Bingo!

Topic: English GCSE revision

List of words:

alliteration	assonance	cliché	colloquial	emotive language
enjambment	juxtapose	list	metaphor	narcissistic
oxymoron	repetition	rhyme	persona	onomatopoeia
rhythm	personification	simile	stanza	rhetorical question

Definitions

Alliteration: *Where a series of words in a sentence begin with the same letter*

Assonance: *Where similar sounds, often vowel sounds, are repeated*

Cliché: *Tired, familiar and hackneyed language*

Colloquial: *Informal language, more often used in speech than in writing*

Emotive language: *Words that provoke strong passions and feelings*

Enjambment: *When a poet ends a line and continues the sentence on the next line*

Juxtapose: *Where two things are put next to each other to create a contrast*

List: *Where a series of things are stated, one after the other*

Metaphor: *Figure of speech where one thing is used to describe another*

Narcissistic: *Describing an author or character who is obsessed with themselves*

Oxymoron: *Where two words go together which do not make logical sense, for example: deafening silence*

Repetition: *Where certain words or phrases are used more than once in order to create an effect*

Rhyme: *Where two words have similar sounds at the end of lines*

Persona: *The voice or character representing a speaker*

Onomatopoeia: *Where words sound like that which they represent*

Rhythm: *The pattern of stresses in speech and written language*

Personification: *Where inanimate objects are given human qualities*

Simile: *A figure of speech where two things are compared*

Stanza: *That which poems are divided up into*

Rhetorical question: *A question which invites no answer*

As soon as a student has crossed off all nine of their words they should shout out: 'Bingo!' You then check their grid and confirm whether or not they have won.

Teacher's tips

As you will note from the example, this activity is excellent for the purposes of revision. As such, it is very useful for lessons leading up to exams or tests – either external or internal to the school.

The activity motivates students to reason backwards – from definitions to words, which is opposite to the usual processes of thought and of learning. In so doing, it leads students to look at words and meanings afresh. This is helpful on three counts: first, it aids in the clarification of definitions; second, it reinforces the connections which students already have in their minds; third, it forces students to think actively about what may have become over-familiar. This final point is important, as over-familiarity can lead to sloppy or incorrect usage based on assumptions or misapprehension.

If you are using the activity with lower-ability students, support them by asking them to work in pairs or groups of three. Students can then discuss the definitions they hear before coming to a conclusion as to which word they apply.

Extensions

- Instead of providing students with the definition of the words, provide them with definitions of the opposites of each word. Students will then have to go through two processes: first, they will have to work out what word applies to the definition; second, they will have to assess of which of the key words this is an antonym.

- Instead of giving a definition for each word, provide an example or something which connects to it. Again, students will have to go through two processes: first, they will have to analyse the example or connected item; second, they will have to work out which of the words this could be signalling.

Development

- Invite a student or a group of students to come to the front of the class and to run the activity in your place. Students should provide definitions of the words just as you would have done. They should also keep track of the words they have covered and, finally, they should check the winner's sheet to see if they really have got a full house.

Plenary 11

Concept map

Students create a map showing what different concepts mean, as well as how they relate to one another.

Materials required: Blank A4 paper, one piece per student; colouring pencils; PowerPoint or IWB slide containing a list of concepts connected to the topic and a set of criteria (see explanation beneath).

Activity

Explain to students that they will be creating a map based around a collection of concepts connected to the area of study. The map should have the following elements:

Concept map elements

- A minimum of five concepts linked to the topic.

- Each concept should be accompanied by a definition and an example.

- Concepts should be connected together with lines, on these lines should be an explanation of how and why they link.

Display these criteria on the board along with ten appropriate concepts. Hand out the sheets of A4 paper and ask students to begin creating their maps. Explain that they can use coloured pencils if they wish, for example, to colour-code the different concepts.

On the next page is an example of a concept map.

Concept map

Topic: Molecular chemistry

List of concepts: atom   element   molecule   electron   neutron

ion   formula   compound   nucleus   covalent bond

Concept map:

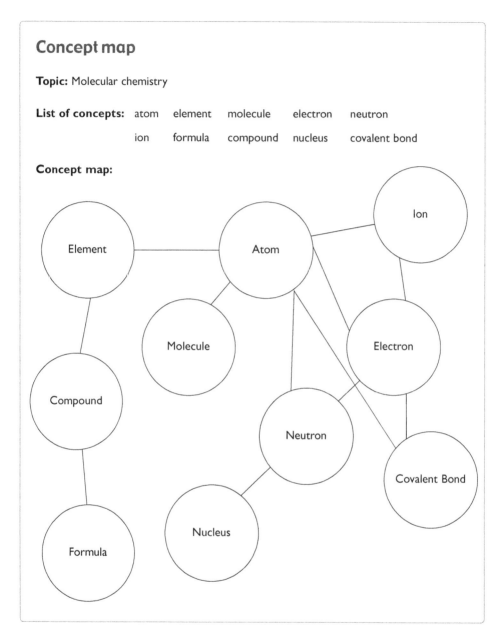

Students will need around ten minutes to complete their maps. Once the time is up, invite them to display their work on their desks and to walk around the room examining that of their peers. They should make a note of two pieces of work they particularly like, along with the reasons why.

Ask students to return to their seats. When everybody is seated, invite three or four students to share their thoughts on the work of their peers with the rest of the group. Give the students whose work is mentioned an opportunity to talk about it as well.

Teacher's tips

A common obstacle with this activity is that, when used for the first time, students can be a little unsure as to how to begin. Avoid this by modelling an example: take two of the concepts and write them on opposite sides of your whiteboard. Ask students to provide you with a definition and an example for each concept and add these to the board. Finally, draw a line between the two concepts and ask students to tell you some of the ways that the two words connect. Write their suggestions above and beneath the line. Having done this once with a class, you will not need to do it again – they will grasp exactly what the activity is asking of them.

A major benefit of this activity is that it provides students with a means by which to visualize the contents of their minds. The maps they create reflect the relationships between ideas that are stored in their heads. Seeing these set down on paper helps students to become aware of the connections and to consider how they might be used or developed in the future.

A final point to note is that the work which students produce can be added to at a later date, and used for revision purposes. The maps they make are working documents which have life beyond the plenary itself.

Extensions

- Ask students to use images to supplement their examples and definitions. These should be drawn and coloured in and ought to either exemplify the words in question or demonstrate some sort of tangential connection.

- Challenge students to make their maps more complex by including a greater number of concepts. Invite them to begin by adding one more concept, along with a definition, an explanation and a series of links. Then, ask them to add another concept, and so on. By adding one concept at a time, students will ensure they deal with each idea separately (otherwise there is a temptation to go for quantity over quality).

Development

- Instead of asking students to produce individual concept maps, ask them to work in groups of three to create large-scale maps. Hand out sheets of A3 paper rather than A4 and invite students to develop their maps in collaboration. Point out that, as each group has three members and a larger sheet of paper, maps should contain more concepts and connections than would be the case if students were working on their own.

Plenary 12

5-5-1

Students summarize their learning and then simplify this not once, but twice.

Materials required: PowerPoint or IWB slide containing task instructions.

Activity

Invite students to write five sentences summarising what they have learnt during the lesson. When they have done this, ask them to share their work with three people sitting close by. Next, invite students to re-write their sentences, taking account of what they have heard from their peers. When this has been done, ask students to repeat the sharing process, but to find three different people with whom to share.

Next, ask students to simplify their five sentences into five key words. Each of these should represent one aspect of the student's learning during the course of the lesson. When this has been done, ask students to stand up and walk around the room. They should share their key words with at least three of their peers. In the process, they should make a note of the words their peers have chosen. When this has been done, ask students to return to their seats. Explain that they should now write a paragraph explaining the similarities and differences between their five key words and the sets of words developed by the peers to whom they spoke.

Finally, invite students to select one word which they feel best sums up their learning during the lesson, or which signifies what they feel is the most important aspect of their learning. Lead a whole-class discussion in which you ask different students to share their words, and in which you encourage students to comment on what their peers have shared.

5-5-1

Example answer, based on the topic The Cause of World War Two

Five Sentences: The Treaty of Versailles put Germany under major economic strain. This strain led to hyperinflation and other problems. In turn, this brought down the Weimar Republic. Hitler came to power as a result. Hitler then went on to start taking over countries in Europe, leading to World War Two.

Five Words: The harsh Treaty of Versailles

One Word: Versailles

Teacher's tips

A great benefit of this activity is that you can make it shorter or longer on the hoof – something which is often necessary when it comes to plenaries. To shorten it, you can miss out the sharing with peers and instead ask students to write five sentences, followed by five key words and then one single word. To lengthen it, you can prolong the discussion at the end, or insert discussions between the other phases (sentences to key words; five key words to one key word).

The activity also provides students with a period in which to reflect on what they have learnt during the lesson. They must do this in order to fulfil the requirements of the task. The process of converting a lesson's worth of learning into five sentences – let alone five key words (or only one) – is complex and requires careful thought and consideration. Through the course of the plenary, students will reinforce their learning and refine their understanding.

Extensions

- Challenge students to communicate their learning in pictures instead of words. Invite them to summarize what they have learnt in five sentences, then to create five pictures which represent these sentences and, finally, to craft a single image which demonstrates what they have learnt.

- Ask students to swap books after they have written their five sentences. Students should read through what their partner has written and then come up with five key words which represent this as accurately as possible. The challenge here is that students will have to think from the perspective of someone else; it may well be the case that their own learning has been slightly – or even altogether – different.

Development

- Use a timer and challenge students to complete the various parts of the activity against the clock. Give just enough time, but no more. This will place students under pressure, creating a mildly tense but exciting atmosphere. Play up the drama of the situation by displaying a countdown timer on your board (do an online search for 'countdown timer').

Plenary 13

Quiz creator

Students become quizmasters and develop quizzes which they can use to test their peers.

Materials required: PowerPoint or IWB slide containing the instructions for the task.

Activity

Explain to students that they are to create a quiz based on the lesson. Here is a selection of methods you might ask them to use:

Quiz creator methods

- Create a ten question quiz based on the lesson.

- Create ten multiple-choice questions based on today's lesson.

- Create a series of quiz questions based on key words and phrases from the topic.

- Pick five pictures connected to the topic. Use these to quiz your peers – can they work out what the pictures represent?

- Create a quiz based on a television quiz show. Your questions should be connected to today's learning.

It is best to specify the format of the quiz as this will ensure continuity across the group and will also help to guide students in coming up with suitable questions.

Give between five and ten minutes for students to create their questions. Some of the quiz types mentioned above will take nearer to ten minutes; some will take nearer to five. When the time is up, divide the class in half.

Invite one set of students to stand up. Explain that they need to partner up with a member of the class who is still sitting down. Upon doing so, they should set about taking it in turns to quiz each other. This should be done alternately, either one question at a time, or one whole quiz at a time.

Lower-ability students often find it helpful to be given a more detailed brief. Below is a criteria you could provide to help them form the questions. You will note that such scaffolding makes it easier for the students to focus on the content of the questions – they do not have to split their thinking between that and the matter of structure.

Question criteria

- Come up with two definition questions.

- Create two multiple-choice questions.

- Create one question which involves an image.

- Create one question which requires an opinion.

Teacher's tips

This activity gets students to go back over everything they have learnt during the course of the lesson in order to create questions which are of a high standard and with which they might be able to catch out their peers. The process involves revisiting and manipulating learning, synthesising a large amount of content and considering how best to communicate thoughts and ideas in a given format. All of this goes a long way towards securing learning in the student's mind.

If students struggle to get going, display a couple of sample questions on the board. Indicate that they should not copy these directly but that they can substitute words and keep the same format in order to get themselves going.

An excellent way to help students develop superior questions works as follows. Walk around the room and look at the questions various students are producing. When you find a good one, share it with the rest of the class, praise the author, and explain exactly why the question is good. This will provide a model which students can use for their own questions. In addition, it will help the class to understand the criteria which need to be met in order for a question to be considered as good.

Extensions

- Challenge students to create more complex, abstract or just plain difficult questions.

- Ask students to create questions which are open-ended and require discursive, reasoned answers. When students are testing each other, encourage them to discuss and debate the answers which are given.

Development

- Split the class in half. Ask the two groups to each create a ten question quiz making use of a variety of different question types and based on the learning from the lesson. Give around ten minutes for this. When the time is up, invite the groups to elect a question-master. This student should leave their group, taking their quiz with them. They should then test the other group before reporting back how well the contestants fared.

Plenary 14

Cross the curriculum

Students make links across the curriculum, connecting what they have learnt to other subjects.

Materials required: Two sets of five cards, each card should contain a different subject from the curriculum; PowerPoint or IWB slide containing instructions for the task.

Activity

Ask students to get into groups of three. Explain that each group will receive a card which has a curriculum subject on it. Display a slide containing the following questions below.

Cross the curriculum questions

- How might you connect what we have learnt today to your subject?

- How might you combine something from your subject with something from today's lesson?

- Why might today's lesson help you in the future in your subject?

Example topic and subject cards:

Topic: Christian ethics

Subject cards: History   English   Geography   Sociology   PE

Example answers:

History: Christian ethics have changed over time. For example, it was once seen as OK to kill people who held different beliefs.

English: Writers such as C.S. Lewis based much of their work on the Christian ethics in which they believed.

Geography: Certain countries are predominantly Catholic, whereas others are predominantly Protestant. Moral codes in these countries are likely to have some differences as a result.

Sociology: The laws by which a country is run might be heavily influenced by the main religion in the country, which could be Christianity.

PE: Whether or not someone cheats when competing could be connected to whether they follow Christian ethics or not.

Invite students to discuss these questions in their group and to make a note of their answers. You should allow about three minutes for this.

When the time is up, ask students to team up with the other group in the class who has been given the same subject. (Two sets of five cards with groups of three works on the assumption that there are 30 students. You will need to adjust the number of cards to suit your class size.) Students should share the results of their discussions, with each set of three taking it in turn to speak. Finally, the whole group should discuss what they think are the best answers to the questions.

To finish the activity, choose two groups and invite them to share their subject and their answers with the rest of the class.

Teacher's tips

This activity is great for helping students to think about the links between subjects and breaks down some of the barriers put in place by the nature of the timetable. In turn, this negates (temporarily) the compartmentalization of knowledge which is a feature of secondary schooling. If used repeatedly, it can help students to see your subject within a broader context.

Try to choose subjects which are not too difficult to link to the topic. With sufficiently creative thinking, nearly anything can be connected. However, it is best to give students a high chance of success so as to avoid disengagement and loss of motivation. This does not mean that you should give the easiest options, just that you should avoid the most unlikely.

Encourage students to analyse what they have done during the course of the lesson. Explain that analysis involves breaking an item up into its constituent parts and that by doing this they will have more starting points from which to try to forge connections and links.

Extensions

- If you have time collect in the cards and redistribute them, making sure that groups receive a subject which differs from their first one and then repeat the activity.

- Challenge students to make connections between the learning and two or three other subjects. Explain that these links should encompass all the separate elements.

- Ask students to create something new – for example, an advert, a poster, a diagram or an invention – which includes something from your lesson and something connected to it from another subject.

Development

- Instead of handing out subject cards, display the five subjects on the board, beneath two of the questions noted in the example. Ask students to work in groups of three. They should attempt to answer both of the questions for all of the subjects in as short a time as possible. The first group to finish should signal to the teacher. They then read out their answers while the whole class listens in. Students are free to challenge anything with which they disagree.

Plenary 15

No to no and no to yes

Students ask each other questions about the lesson, but no one is allowed to use the words 'yes' or 'no'.

Materials required: A PowerPoint or IWB slide displaying the instructions for the task.

Activity

Explain to students that they will be working in pairs. Each student will need to come up with ten questions based on the lesson. These questions can be closed or open and they can also be supplemented by follow-up questions. Indicate that students will be using their questions to test their partners, but that there is a twist: When answering, students are not allowed to use the words 'yes' or 'no'.

Give the class around five minutes to come up with their questions. You can support them in any of the following ways:

• Display some exemplar questions on the board.

• Walk around the room looking at students' work. When you see a good question, read it out, praise the student and explain to the rest of the class why the question is noteworthy.

• Display a list on the board made up of different aspects of the lesson. Indicate to students that they can use this list to structure their questions. For example, they could choose three of the items and come up with three questions based on each of these.

When the time is up, ask students to get into pairs and to decide who will be person 'A' and who will be person 'B'. Indicate that person 'A' will ask their questions first, and that person 'B' must try to answer them without using the words 'yes' or 'no'. Give three minutes for this. When the time is up, ask the pairs to swap roles and to repeat the activity.

It is up to you whether you make the game competitive or not. If you do, you should ask pairs to keep track of how many times the words 'yes' or 'no' are said. The student in each pair who uses these words the fewest times is the winner.

Teacher's tips

When students are taking it in turns to ask each other questions, walk around the room and listen in to the answers which are given. Theatrically point out moments when 'yes' or 'no' are used. This will help to create an air of fun and drama; it will also help to sharpen student's minds, drawing their attention to the task of spotting mistakes.

This activity is good for developing listening skills. When students are giving their answers, their partner has to listen very carefully to what it is they are saying. In order to ascertain whether or not the words 'yes' and 'no' have been used, they will need to carefully scan every word, checking its form and content.

Another benefit of this activity is that it encourages students to think at length about what they studied during the course of the lesson. This is because they will be trying to develop questions with which to catch out their partners – luring them into mistakenly saying 'yes' or 'no'. The whole process will help to reinforce the learning in students' minds.

Finally, it is worth pointing out that some students may not understand the task when first explained. This tends to be down to the negative element of the instructions (don't say 'yes' or 'no') which is harder to process, and can sometimes lead to confusion. To avoid problems arising, create three sample questions and invite a student to ask them to you. Answer them in the correct manner – highlighting to students as you do so why this is correct in the context of the task.

Extension

• Further limit students' options for answering. You might like to prohibit key words from the lesson or common words such as 'the' or 'and'.

• Challenge a student who has shown themselves to be adept at answering to come to the front of the class. Invite the rest of the class to ask their toughest questions to the student. See how long they can go on giving correct answers while also avoiding the words 'yes' and 'no'.

Development

• Put students into groups of four. Explain that each group is a team and that they will be taking on another team in a challenge match. Students should work in their groups to come up with ten taxing questions they could ask their opponents. Give around five minutes for this. When the time is up, invite groups to pair up. Teams then take it in turns to ask each other questions; they also keep track of who uses the words 'yes' and 'no' the greatest number of times.

Plenary 16

Labelling

Students work individually or in a team to label a diagram or picture connected to the lesson.

Materials required: A class set of handouts, there should be an equal number of five different unlabelled images.

Activity

Provide each student in the class with a diagram or picture connected to the topic of the preceeding lesson, for example if the lesson was about osmosis you could find five different pictures of osmosis happening. You should print as many copies as you need of five different images and distribute these at random. Ask students to use their knowledge to annotate their image. Tell them that they should specify what different elements are and provide explanations of what their function is, as well as their relationship to other aspects of the whole. Give around five minutes for this section of the plenary. When the time is up, invite students to form groups of three. Each group should have at least two different images. Ask students to take it in turns to share their annotations with the rest of their group.

Teacher's tips

This plenary is great for lessons that include a diagrammatic or visual element. However, it can also be used with learning that does not contain either of these. For example, an English lesson focussing on a play could give rise to a picture of a scene from that play, or a diagram showing the relationships between different characters. In both cases, students would be able to label these by calling on the knowledge and understanding developed during the course of the lesson.

A benefit of this activity is that it encourages students to apply what they know to a concrete setting. This means that abstract ideas can be contextualized and exemplified and this will help reinforce learning.

If you feel that some students will struggle to label their diagrams, provide a list of key terms. Explain that these are appropriate for the image in question, but that it is up to students to work out which applies to which part.

Extensions

- When students have finished labelling their image, present them with a second image. This should either be a close-up of some aspect of the first image, or a picture showing the first image in some sort of context. The challenge is that students must reassess their choices and methods given the different realising of the item in question. In so doing, they should come to accurately label the second image.

- Give students further criteria to include in their labelling. For example: alternative name for the element; where else might the element be found?; how important is the element overall?

Developments

- Divide the class into groups of five. Display an image on the board. Give each group a sheet of A2 paper. Explain that students must work together to recreate the image on their paper, and that they must also label it. Indicate that labelling should extend beyond naming different elements of the image. It should also include explanations of functions, relationships and purposes. Give ten minutes for this section of the plenary. When the time is up, invite each group to share what they have created with the rest of the class.

- Follow the previous method, except give each group a single part of the image to reproduce and annotate. When the whole class has finished, invite the groups to clear a space in the middle of the room and to then slot their separate sections together. Ask one member of each group to talk through their particular part. Conclude by asking a selection of students to comment on the strengths and limitations of the final piece of work.

Plenary 17

Hot-seating

Students are put in the hot-seat and must answer questions about the lesson while everyone else watches.

Materials required: A chair placed at the front of the class in a position for all to see – this is the hot-seat; a PowerPoint or IWB slide containing the instructions for the task.

Activity

You can run this plenary in one of two ways:

1. Divide the class into groups with four students in each group. Explain that, after five minutes, one member of each group will be selected at random. They will then go into the 'hot-seat'. Before this happens, students should work individually to come up with a series of taxing questions based on the topic of the preceeding lesson. When five minutes have passed, ask students to number themselves one to four in their groups. Select one of these numbers at random and indicate that whoever has chosen that number is now in the hot-seat. The rest of the group have three minutes in which to ask that person their questions about the lesson. When the time is up, pick another number and ask group members to swap round and repeat the activity.

2. Give the class five minutes in which to come up with a series of taxing questions connected to the lesson. Indicate that students should work in pairs and that they should make a note of their best questions. When the time is up, invite a member of the class to come to the front. They are in the hot-seat and will have to answer questions posed by their peers. (Select the student by asking for volunteers, through a random method or based on an assumption about who is likely to perform well in the hot-seat.) Choose one of five or six pairs to ask questions. When this has been done, praise the student in the hot-seat for their efforts and ask them to swap with another student. Repeat the process as many times as you wish.

Teacher's tips

A good way to create drama in this activity is through playing appropriate music as the student comes up to the hot-seat. On YouTube you can find a variety of television quiz show themes, you could use one of these to heighten the theatricality and to engage the class.

If following method two, try to avoid selecting students who find talking in front of the class difficult. In this plenary, the onus is very much on the student sitting in the hot-seat. It is therefore not particularly good for students who are shy or nervous when speaking to a large audience. Should you have a number of students in your class for who this is an issue, opt for method one.

Encourage discussion and debate in the class when the student in the hot-seat gives their answers. This talk should focus on whether students agree with what is being said. If they do not, they should indicate what they think the correct answer is and why.

A final point to note is that you might want to have a go in the hot-seat yourself. If you choose to, indicate to students that this is going to happen and invite them to come up with questions which they believe you will not be able to answer. A session can then ensue in which the class is trying to beat the teacher – this will be fun for all involved (I assure you!).

Extensions

- Give students specific areas about which to ask questions. Tailor these to suit individual students. For example, if a student is particularly knowledgeable about one area of the topic, but knows less about another area, ask them to construct questions based on the latter. This will be challenging and will also cause the student to widen their repertoire.

- Give students specific types of questions which they must construct. For example: open questions based around arguments; questions which reference a statement connected to the learning; or, questions which could be answered in a number of different ways.

Development

- Divide the class into groups of four. Ask students to work in their teams to come up with five thoughtful, challenging questions based on the learning. Give them five minutes in which to do this. When the time is up, choose one team at random to come to the front. All four of those students are in the hot-seat. The remaining groups get to ask one question in turn. Students work as a team to answer the questions.

Plenary 18

You're bard!

Students must channel the poetic muse in order to recreate an aspect of their learning in verse form.

Materials required: A PowerPoint or IWB slide containing instructions for the task; examples of the poetical form(s) you want students to use.

Activity

Ask students to work in pairs to create a mind-map of everything they have learnt during the course of the lesson. When they have done this, ask them to add anything else they know about what they have already written down.

Next, explain to students that they will be using their mind-maps to create a poem about some aspect of the lesson. Display a PowerPoint or IWB slide containing instructions to that effect, as well as one or more examples of the poetic form(s) you would like students to use. The following forms are most apt:

Best types of poems

- Limerick: this is a five-line poem in which the first, second and fifth lines share a rhyme, as do the third and fourth lines, so the rhyming form is: AABBA. Limericks are usually humorous.

- Rhyming couplets: these are two consecutive lines which share a rhyme. A poem could contain any number of rhyming couplets. A six-line poem would be of the rhyming form: AABBCC

- Haiku: this is a three-line poem. The first and third lines have five syllables and the second line has seven.

- Acrostic: this is a poem where each line begins with a letter which, when written out in order, spell the word which the poem is about.

You can find example of all these poetic forms on the internet or you can make your own. There are also examples of each of these types of poems in the box on the next page.

Give students five minutes in which to create their poems. Indicate that they can work individually or in pairs – the choice is theirs. When the time is up, invite a selection of students to share their work with the rest of the class. Ensure there is an atmosphere of goodwill and collegiality – praise and applaud each poet after they have read out their work.

You're bard!

Topic: The Cuban missile crisis

Haiku:
The missile crisis
Was a turning point, though not
For *all* those involved.

Limerick:
There once was a Cuban crisis,
That threatened to be quite divisive,
But all was OK,
When Pres' JFK,
Thought negotiatin' would be decisive.

Rhyming Couplets:
The whole wide world was racked with fear,
When in 1962 war came near,
Many thought disaster was close at hand,
And rejoiced when missiles left Cuban land.

Acrostic:
J – John Kennedy was leader of his nation
F – For thirteen days there was confrontation
K – Khrushchev and he talked to end the situation

Teacher's tips

If students are struggling to produce a poem, give them the range of poetical forms from which to choose. This opens the activity up and allows students to have a freer hand in creating something which is appropriate.

A good way to create pace and to help students to engage with the task is to write a poem yourself during the course of the plenary. As you go about this, share your work with students who are struggling or who are finding the activity difficult. Your ideas will act as a model, helping students to develop their own work and to engage with the task.

One of the great benefits of this plenary is that students create their own memory aides.

Poems, particularly those which rhyme, are often memorable so students will write verses which will stick in their minds well beyond the end of the lesson. You may find that these are returned to again and again during the course of a topic, or when revision time comes around.

If students are reluctant to share their poems with the rest of the class, there are two options open to you. First, you can offer to read the poem on behalf of the student. This way, you are taking the onus off them but still ensuring that their work is heard and praised. Second, you might like to ask students to get into groups of five and to share their poems with each other in this smaller setting.

Extensions

- Challenge students to write a second verse or to write a second poem using a different poetical form.

- Invite students to create a second poem or verse based around a specific aspect of the learning. You can choose something which is verbally cumbersome or which is difficult to rhyme as a way of further challenging their thinking.

Development

- When students have created their poems, invite half of the class to stand up and the other half to remain seated. Explain that the students who are standing up have been tasked with hearing as many of the poems as possible which their seated peers have created, inside three minutes. Signal for them to begin and then, when the time is up, ask the two halves to swap over and to repeat the process.

Plenary 19

Sculpture vulture

Students create sculptures which represent aspects of their learning.

Materials required: Something students can use to create sculptures, such as building bricks, play dough, a collection of used materials such as cereal boxes, bits of string, egg boxes and so on; a PowerPoint or IWB slide containing the instructions for the task.

Activity

Ask students to work in pairs to create a mind-map based on the lesson. Give two minutes for this. When the time is up, explain that students will be working with their partner to produce a sculpture which represents one aspect of their learning. Indicate that students can either choose something from their mind-map, or decide on something else entirely. The only requisite is that it must be connected to the lesson.

Hand out the sculpture materials (see above) and explain that students have five minutes in which to create their piece of artwork. You may choose to provide success criteria at this point, or you may prefer to leave the activity entirely open. The choice is yours and will depend largely on how confident you are in the abilities of your students. If you opt for the first option, here are a sample set of success criteria:

Sculpture success criteria

- Ensure your sculpture represents something from today's lesson.

- Include at least one symbolic element in your sculpture.

- Prepare an explanation of your sculpture (that you could give to an audience).

When the time is up, ask students to stop what they are doing and to place their sculptures at the end of their desks. Split the class in half. Ask one group of students to leave their seats and to walk around the room examining the sculptures. The rest of the class remain seated and they should explain the meaning behind their sculptures to anyone who comes for a viewing. Give two minutes for this part of the activity. When the time is up, ask the class to swap over and to repeat the process.

Teacher's tips

Encourage students to choose abstract and conceptual elements of the lesson as the basis of their sculptures. This will lead to particularly innovative and thought-provoking work. In addition, students will have to analyse the ideas they have been working with at length. Only by doing this will they be able to develop sculptures which accurately convey the meaning of these aspects of their learning.

As you will note, the activity gets students to think carefully about what they have learnt. Creating a sculpture is a difficult challenge which is made all the more taxing by the fact that it has to represent something specific from the lesson. During the course of the plenary, students engage in a whole series of cognitive processes which help to reinforce what they have learnt.

During the final part of the plenary, when students are displaying their work to one another, walk around the room and take part in the gallery experience. Comment on the sculptures, praise them, ask questions and listen to students' explanations. This will positively reinforce the work students have done, further develop their thinking, and allow you to elicit information about their knowledge and understanding of the topic.

Extensions

- Instead of allowing students to choose what they are going to represent through their sculptures, choose it for them. This way, you can opt for challenging ideas, concepts, processes and so on. Students will have to think more deeply in order to convey these through sculpture.

- Use more stringent success criteria. For example: You must include a series of geometric shapes; your sculpture must be in multiple parts; you must make your sculpture difficult to interpret but not impossible.

Development

- Divide the class into groups of five and assign each group an aspect of the lesson which they have to sculpt. Invite the groups to create large sculptures using the materials on hand. Indicate that these should cover a variety of different elements connected to the group's particular aspect. When sculptures have been completed, ask each group in turn to showcase and explain their work to the rest of the class.

Plenary 20

Advertising campaign

Students use advertising techniques to try and 'sell' what they have learnt in the lesson.

Materials required: A PowerPoint or IWB slide containing the instructions for the task; example adverts (optional – see below).

Activity

Explain to students they are going to advertise what they have learnt during the course of the lesson. If you have time, show students some examples of adverts and talk them through the key features such as design, language and product placement. At this point, there are three options open to you. They work as follows:

1. Divide the class into groups of three. Explain that each group is to produce a television commercial 'selling' the learning from the lesson. Give students ten minutes in which to develop a 30-second advert. Ensure that you are strict with the time. Students should spend no more than five minutes planning and preparing their advert. The rest of the time should be spent in rehearsal. When the ten minutes is up, invite groups to join up with two other teams. They then take it in turns to show each other their adverts.

2. Students work individually. Explain that each student should choose three things they have learnt in the lesson and use these as the basis of a poster advertisement. Indicate the audience for the finished work is students in a primary school. Give ten minutes for the completion of the poster. At the end of this time, invite students to stand up and walk around the room with their posters. They should share their work with at least three of their peers.

3. Ask students to work in pairs. Explain that each pair should come up with a slogan and a jingle advertising some aspect of the lesson. Give five minutes for this. When the time is up, ask pairs to team up with two or three other pairs. In these new, larger groups, each pair should take it in turn to share their work. When everybody has had a chance, the larger groups should split up and new ones should form. The sharing of the work is then repeated.

Teacher's tips

Whichever method you choose here, students will be compelled to think carefully about their learning. They will have to go back over what has been done in the lesson and consider what elements they can pull out and advertise. Furthermore, once they have done this they will have to manipulate that information so that it fits within the constraints of the particular medium. This will again see them thinking carefully about their learning. In the process, they will reinforce their knowledge and understanding.

There is an added incentive in this plenary which gets students to give deep consideration to how they present their learning – that is, the need to ensure it conforms to the norms of advertising. Students must not just convey what they have learnt, they must sell it. In so doing, they will be trying to persuade the viewer to seek it out for themselves. Thinking in this way will make students consider the benefits, uses and purposes of what they have learnt. This, in turn, will further reinforce their learning. At the same time, it will broaden their understanding through the crafting of new connections and links.

If time is of the essence, you can truncate the whole process by asking students to come up with three advertising 'headlines'. Explain that these should be three statements persuasively expressing the benefits of the key elements of the lesson. Including sharing with a partner and a brief whole-class discussion, this can be done effectively inside seven minutes.

Extensions

- Challenge students to create a cross-media advertising campaign. This will involve adverts in more than one medium. For example, students might develop a radio advert, a television advert and a marketing email.

- When students have completed their adverts, ask them to imagine how they would have done things differently given an alternative audience. Students should write a paragraph outlining their thoughts.

Development

- Split the class into five groups and ask each group to develop a television advert based on a certain aspect of the lesson. Display a set of success criteria and indicate that the whole process is a competitive one; all the adverts will be judged by the teacher and a winner will be announced. Give the groups between five and ten minutes in which to develop their work and then ask each in turn to give the class a run through of what they have produced. Use the success criteria to help judge which is the winner.

Plenary 21

Assessment for learning

Use the plenary to elicit information from your students about what stage they have reached in their learning.

Materials required: *Method 2*: enough slips of paper for every student in the class; *Method 3*: a series of PowerPoint or IWB slides containing questions about the lesson; *Method 4*: a series of PowerPoint or IWB slides containing a continuum and a series of statements connected to the lesson; *Method 5*: a class set of mini-whiteboards.

Activity

Assessment for learning involves three things: eliciting information from students about their learning, opening up success criteria for students, and providing formative feedback to help them make progress. You can use a plenary to achieve the first of these aims. Here are five different methods:

1. Ask students to use their thumbs to show you where they are at either in relation to the learning in general, or to a series of questions related to the learning. 'Thumbs up' = I feel good/I understand. 'Thumbs in the middle' = I feel OK/I think I understand but am not certain. 'Thumbs down' = I am not happy with this/I do not understand.

2. Hand each student a slip of paper. Display a question on the board related to the lesson. Explain that all students must write their answer on their paper and then hand this in on the way out of the classroom.

3. Create five slides, each containing a different question about the lesson. Provide four possible answers for each question. Indicate that the corners of the room represent the numbers 1–4. On displaying each question, invite students to stand in the corner of the room which signifies the answer they think is correct. Develop discussions where appropriate.

4. Display a continuum on the board ranging from 'strongly agree' to 'strongly disagree'. Display a series of statements above the continuum, each connected to the lesson. Ask students to stand up and explain that upon each statement being revealed they should move to the point on the continuum which reflects their position on the matter. Develop discussions as appropriate.

5. Hand out a set of mini-whiteboards. Pose a series of questions to students, each connected to the lesson. Ask students to write or draw their answers on the mini-whiteboards and then to hold these up for all to see. Develop discussions as appropriate.

Here is an example of method 3:

Assessment for learning

Topic: Algebra

Instructions: The four corners of the room represent the numbers 1–4, starting from the door and working clockwise. For each question, go to the corner which represents the answer you think is correct.

Sample question: $2x^2 = y$

If $Y = 8$, which of the following can x not be?

1) 2   2) –2   3) 1   4) 3

Clue: There may be more than one correct answer

Teacher's tips

Using assessment for learning techniques as the basis of a plenary means that you can leave a lesson with a clear sense of where students in your class are in their learning. The information can then be used in your future planning, helping you to tailor your lessons more closely to their needs.

If you have noticed a misconception cropping up repeatedly during the course of a lesson, or if you feel a certain part of the lesson was generally poorly received, alter your plenary accordingly so that it focuses on this. Any of the five methods outlined above can be adapted at a moment's notice. This will allow you to ascertain whether what you have sensed or felt is actually the case.

Extensions

- In methods 3, 4 and 5, there is scope for developing discussions. These should involve students explaining the reasoning behind the choices they have made. Do not be afraid to push students in order to get them to give a full and detailed explanation of their reasoning. Use careful questioning, counter-examples and alternative suggestions as a means to do this.

- If using method 1, ask students who understand the work or the question to explain it to their peers. You might do this through asking students to pair up once the thumbs have been shown, or by asking a student who has their thumb up to explain to the whole class.

Development

- In method 2, instead of asking students to write an answer to a question, ask them to note down one question they would like to know the answer to, based on what they have learnt. Use these questions to ascertain where the gaps in the class's knowledge lie and also as the basis of your next lesson with them.

Plenary 22

Extra! Extra!

Students turn their learning into a newspaper front page.

Materials required: A class set of A4 handouts, each of which should look like the front page of a newspaper minus the content, there should be an empty box with space for a headline, three empty columns with space for writing and an empty box with space for a picture; a PowerPoint or IWB slide containing instructions, success criteria and questions (see below).

Activity

Explain to students that they are going to create a newspaper front page about their learning. Ask the class to get into pairs and then distribute the blank newspaper frames. Indicate that students should pick a key aspect of their learning or of the lesson, and that this should form the basis of their front page.

Give the class five minutes in which to fill in the handout. Provide a set of success criteria such as the following:

Extra! Extra! success criteria

- Create a snappy headline which grabs the reader's attention.

- Write the opening paragraph of your story and then sketch out what would go in the remainder of the piece. Write more if you have time.

- Draw an image which represents something connected to your story.

When the time is up, ask pairs to get into groups of eight (four pairs joining together). In these new groups, each pair should take it in turns to talk through their filled-in front page. Put the following questions on the board as a structure for students to follow:

Extra! Extra! questions

- How did you decide on your story?

- What are the key features of your story?

- How have you made the story suitable for a newspaper format?

Give each pair a minute. When the overall time is up, invite each group to nominate one pair whose front page was particularly good and to share it with the rest of the class.

Teacher's tips

This plenary encourages students to revisit everything they have learnt during the course of a lesson, and to view it from the perspective of whether or not it could be turned into a newspaper story. By engaging in this process, students will be analysing and assessing everything they have learnt. This will result in two things: first, it will reinforce their learning, leading to stronger and more powerful memories; second, it will cause students to develop a clearer sense of what exactly goes to make up their learning – they will become more aware of its constituents, as well as the wider whole.

It is easy to adapt this plenary to different time constraints. If you have a lot of time, invite students to write more of their article, instead of sketching out the general points. If you do not have a lot of time, you could even do away with the handouts and instead ask students to come up with a headline, three key bullet points for the article, and a sketch of an image.

A nice way of sharing the work that every student has done is, at the end of the plenary, to go round each pair in turn, starting from the front of the class and working backwards, and ask them to read aloud their headline. This is sufficiently short to be manageable, but still affords all students the chance to have their ideas heard by the rest of the class.

Extensions

- Challenge students to write a how-to guide as part of their front page piece. This should explain to the reader how to use some aspect of the learning from the lesson.

- Ask students to create a series of images showing different things that they have learnt. This will require a different type of handout, or students can do it in their books.

Development

- Divide the class into groups of five. Give each group a sheet of A2 paper and some felt-tip pens. Display a newspaper front page on the board as an example. Ask students to create their own front pages, in their groups, using the A2 paper. Indicate that they can copy the layout and structure from the example on the board. Give groups ten minutes to complete this. When the time is up, invite each group in turn to come to the front of the class and to share their work with their peers.

Plenary 23

Exam questions

Students use their learning to answer exam questions based on the lesson.

Materials required: A PowerPoint or IWB slide containing instructions and exam-style questions; a mark-scheme or set of success criteria (optional – see below).

Activity

Explain to students that they will be using their learning to help them answer exam-style questions. At this point, there are three options open to you:

1. Ask students to work in pairs. Display an example of an exam question on the board. Talk the class through how it is structured. Then, invite students to work in their pairs to create two of their own exam-style questions. These should be based on some aspect of the lesson. Give around three minutes for this. When the time is up, ask pairs to team up with another duo and to swap questions. They should then take three minutes to discuss how they would go about answering these. Finally, thoughts should be shared between the pairs in a brief discussion.

2. Display a slide containing three exam-style questions. Divide the class into three sections. Indicate that each section of students will be attempting a different question. Specify which one this will be. Give students five minutes in which to develop an answer (this may need to be a plan or bullet points, it will depend on the type of questions you use). When the time is up, ask students to get into groups of three. These should contain one student from each section. Give groups five minutes in which to share their work and to discuss the differences between the various questions.

3. Display a slide containing three exam-style questions. Ask students to work in pairs. Give each pair a handout containing the mark-scheme or success criteria relevant to the questions you have displayed. Invite students to select one of the three questions and to create a model answer (or a plan of one depending on the type of question). They should use the mark-scheme or success criteria to help them do this. Allow between five and ten minutes for this. When the time is up, select three or four pairs and ask them to share their work with the class.

Here is an example of the activity, based on method 3:

Exam questions

Topic: Sociology of the family

Instructions: Work with a partner. Choose one of the three questions and create a model answer. Use the mark-scheme to help you.

Questions:

- 'The family has the most influence on an individual's behaviour.' Evaluate the arguments for and against this claim.

- 'Symmetrical families are the norm in the contemporary UK.' Evaluate the arguments for and against this claim.

- 'How you do at school depends on what your family is like.' Evaluate the arguments for and against this claim.

Teacher's tips

If you are working with a GCSE or A Level class, this activity is an excellent way to contextualize what has been learnt during the lesson in regard to the examinations. Students must apply their learning so as to create or answer questions which reflect the realities of assessment. The whole process brings about two significant benefits: first, it gives students first-hand experience of what their final exams will be like; second, it causes students to manipulate their learning so as to make it fit the demands of the exam questions. Not only will this reinforce their knowledge and understanding, it will provide good practice as well.

If you have students in your class who struggle with exam technique, use this as an opportunity to work with them. Once the class are on task, talk to those students who are having problems and provide them with simple structures or methods which they can follow so as to make things easier.

Encouraging students to use mark-schemes or success criteria (as in method 3) is always good. It helps them to become aware of what they will be judged against. As a result, it will be easier for them to do that which is being expected of them.

Extensions

- If using method 1, challenge pairs to create a model answer for the question. Explain that once they have produced this, they should annotate it as well. The notes should highlight the different aspects of the work which, when added together, make it into a model answer.

- If using method 2, ask students to sketch out possible answer to the other two questions, once they have finished answering their own.

Development

- Take six sheets of A2 paper and write a different exam question connected to the lesson at the top of each one. Distribute these around the room. Invite students to walk around and to look at all the questions. Indicate that they should add their thoughts about how to answer underneath. Give around five minutes for this. When the time is up, split the class into six groups. Give each group one of the sheets of paper. Ask them to summarize what has been written. Finally, go round the groups in turn and ask them to share their summary with the rest of the class.

Plenary 24

Neighbours

Students work with their neighbour to review the lesson.

Materials required: A PowerPoint or IWB slide containing the instructions for the task and some sample questions.

Activity

Explain to students that they will be working with the person sat next to them to review the lesson. Display a slide containing the following questions:

Neighbours questions

- What three things has your neighbour learnt today?

- What would your neighbour like to know more about?

- What does your neighbour think about X (insert something from the lesson here)?

- What conclusion has your neighbour drawn about today's lesson?

- How might your neighbour change the lesson?

Tell the class that each student will be interviewing their partner using these questions.

Invite students to get into their pairs. Ask for each duo to label themselves as 'A' and 'B'. Explain that the students who are 'A' will be asking the questions first. They should make notes as they go through and their aim is to build up a detailed picture of what their partner thinks about the lesson. Give between three and five minutes for this. When the time is up, ask students to swap roles and to repeat the process.

Conclude the activity by asking a number of different pairs to share their thoughts with the whole class. This should be a cumulative discussion in which each contributor adds to what has been said. There is no need for questioning, analysis or evaluation. The whole process is one of review and the sharing of thoughts.

Here is an example of the activity:

Neighbours

Topic: The human skeleton

- What three things has your neighbour learnt about the human skeleton today?

- What would your neighbour like to know more about relating to the human skeleton?

- What does your neighbour think about the way in which bones mend?

- What conclusions has your neighbour drawn about the human skeleton as a result of today's lesson?

- How might your neighbour change the lesson to find out more about the human skeleton?

Teacher's tips

Everyone likes to be asked what they think; this plenary plays on that fact. Students will be encouraged to talk and to share their thoughts on the lesson when you use it. This will lead to a positive, focussed atmosphere in the room and a sense of collaboration both within pairs and across the class as a whole.

By providing students with a list of questions, you will be achieving two specific ends. First, you will ensure that conversations cover exactly what you would like them to cover. For example, you might use question three from above to focus on a certain aspect of the learning which you feel deserves to be revisited. Second, you will be helping students to get into the task more easily than might otherwise be the case. If you do not provide any questions, students may well find it difficult to sustain an interview for any length of time.

The final point to note is that the whole process of review, which this plenary revolves around, sees students thinking carefully about two things: first, the actual content of the lesson – what has been studied and what has been learnt; second, their own feelings about the lesson – what they think and why they think it.

Extensions

- Challenge students to come up with their own set of questions either as a supplement to yours, or as a replacement. When they have done this, they should use them to interview their partner.

- Ask students to probe more deeply into their partner's answers. This will involve asking further questions, focussing on what it is that they have said.

Development

- When pairs have finished their interviews, invite them to team up with another duo. These new groups of four should spend a few minutes sharing the findings of their earlier questioning sessions. They should then create a brief summary pulling together what they think are the most interesting and the most important things to come out of the interviews. When the time is up, invite a selection of groups to share these summaries with the rest of the class.

Plenary 25

Random feedback

Students are chosen at random to give feedback on their learning during the lesson.

Materials required: A PowerPoint or IWB slide containing instructions for the task; for method 1, a PowerPoint document as described below; for method 2, a collection of slips of paper and an opaque bag, as described below.

Activity

Explain to students that you will be selecting people at random to feed back to the rest of the class. Indicate that students should take a minute to reflect silently on what they have learnt and what they have done during the course of the lesson. Suggest that everyone in the class should note down a short list of bullet points reflecting their thoughts. When the time is up, use one of the following three methods to choose students at random:

1. Enter the names of all your students onto a PowerPoint document, one name per slide. Set the slide transition counter to '0' and to automatic. Tick the box marked 'Loop'. When you play the slide show, all the slides will whizz through at speed. Simply press the escape button on your keyboard (esc) to make the show stop and to select a student.

2. Give each student a number, starting from one and working up until you reach the end of the class. Write down the same set of numbers on small slips of paper, one number per slip. Place these in an opaque bag. Withdraw a slip at random and read out the number. The corresponding student has to share their thoughts.

3. Write down a number between one and 100. Keep this secret. Ask your students to do the same and then to reveal their choices. The student(s) whose number is closest to your own are the first to share their thoughts.

In each case, you can continue using the method so as to ensure that you pick contributors at random.

You could display the following questions to help students with their answers:

> ## Random feedback questions
>
> - What is the most important thing you have learnt this lesson?
>
> - What do you know now that you did not know at the start of the lesson?
>
> - How might you alter today's lesson? Why?

After each student has shared their thoughts, ask two other students to comment on what they have heard. These contributions should involve a reflection in which the students talk about whether they agree or disagree with their peer, whether they were surprised by what they heard, and whether they themselves have something different they would like to say. In essence, you will be developing a group discussion off the back of the random feedback.

> ## Teacher's tips
>
> Random feedback has two major benefits: first, it ensures that all students are engaged with the task, this is because students know that they are as likely as anyone else to be asked to share their thoughts; second, it prevents you unconsciously selecting certain students to answer as the method is random selection. Therefore, it gives everyone in the class an equal chance of being asked to speak.
>
> You might want to insert a short addition between the silent reflection and the random feedback. This should be as follows. Invite students to share their thoughts and their bullet points with the person sat next to them. Give between 30 seconds and a minute for this. The purpose of such an addition is to put students at ease. Having had the opportunity to talk, and having had the silence in the class broken, students will be more comfortable and confident in sharing their thoughts through the random feedback mechanism.

Extensions

- Use questioning to push students' thinking. When they have shared their thoughts, ask them to expand, to clarify, to assess or to analyse that which they have said.

- Challenge students to evaluate their own participation in the lesson as well as the lesson itself (in an overall sense). They should note down the strengths and weaknesses they identify and be ready to share these with the whole class during the random feedback section of the plenary.